In Search of Israel

In Search of Israel

Batya Ruth Wootten

In Search of Israel

Copyright © 1988 by Batya Ruth Wootten

Published and distributed by Destiny Image, P.O. Box 351, Shippensburg, PA 17257
Distributed by House Of David, Box 777, Lakewood, New York 14750.
ISBN 0-914903-56-X
Printed in the United States of America.
All quotes are used by permission.

Unless otherwise noted, all Scripture quotations are taken from the New American Standard Bible. Copyright © The Lockman Foundation 1960, 1962, 1963, 1968, 1971, 1972, 1973, 1975, 1977. Published by Holman Bible Publishers.

Verses marked TAB are taken from The Amplified Bible. Copyright © 1964 by the Zondervan Publishing House; and © 1958 by the Lockman Foundation.

Verses marked ATS are taken from the ArtScroll Tanach Series. Copyright © 1977, 1980 by Mesorah Publications, Ltd. Published by Mesorah Publications, Ltd.

Verses marked KJV are taken from the King James Version of the Bible.

Verses marked NIV are taken from the New International Version. Copyright © 1973, 1978, 1984 by International Bible Society. Published by Zondervan Publishing House.

Verses marked TNKH are taken from the Tanakh, A New Translation of The Holy Scriptures (Traditional Hebrew Text). Copyright © 1985. Published by The Jewish Publication Society.

Note: In some Scripture quotations the author has used italics, or the translator's alternate word choice for emphasis.

To my Father in Heaven.
I asked and He answered.

BEHOLD, I WILL TAKE THE STICK OF JOSEPH, WHICH IS IN THE HAND OF EPHRAIM, AND THE TRIBES OF ISRAEL, HIS COMPANIONS; AND I WILL PUT THEM WITH IT, WITH THE STICK OF JUDAH, AND MAKE THEM ONE STICK, AND THEY WILL BE ONE IN MY HAND (EZEKIEL 37:19).

Acknowledgments

There are many who are to be acknowledged in the writing of this book. First and foremost is my husband, Angus, who constantly encouraged me and who made it possible for me to study. I also wish to acknowledge my children, whose lives God used to help me see many truths about His children.

I am indebted to Ephraim and Rimona Frank. Rimona's knowledge as an editor of Hebrew was a great asset to me. David Bivin, Hebrew teacher, scholar and co-author of *Fluent Biblical and Modern Hebrew* and *The Difficult Words of Jesus*, was most valuable in his critique.

I am appreciative of the help of many friends, especially Clara del Mar, who typed and retyped without complaint for three years.

CONTENTS

1
WHO IS ISRAEL?

❧ Under the canopy of a star-lit sky, a man and an angelic being wrestled. Ultimately the whole world would be affected by the match that took place in this quiet gorge. The audience, the heavenly host, looked on in awe as the two rolled vigorously in the dust, limbs intertwined like a vine.

Jacob clung tenaciously to the angelic being. Mysteriously, the angel could not overcome the human being, and yet he had the power to dislocate Jacob's hip with a touch. After wrestling all night, the angel said, " 'Let me go, for it is daybreak.' But Jacob replied, 'I will not let you go unless you bless me.' The man asked him, 'What is your name?' 'Jacob,' he answered" (Genesis 32:26-27, NIV).

The angelic being replied, " 'No longer will it be said that your name is Jacob, but Israel, for you have striven with the

Divine and with human and have overcome'....and he blessed him there" (Genesis 32:29-30, ATS)

Israel—a name given as a blessing. But who is the heir of this blessing? To whom does it rightfully belong?

For two thousand years following God's call of Jacob—though divided into two houses—the twelve tribes of Israel appeared to be Jacob's heirs. Then, in Israel, a Son was born. He was fond of calling himself the Son of Man. However, He was a man with many names: the Lamb of God, the Son of David, the Good Shepherd, the Glory of Israel. Paradoxically, the life and death of this Prince of Peace divided Israel once again.

Another war began in Israel—a battle for the title of Israel. For 1900 years this conflict has continued, pitting brother against brother and bringing grief to the heart of the Father.

Today, two peoples—the adherents of Christianity and the adherents of Judaism—lay claim to the coveted title of Israel. These two peoples declare themselves to be the true heirs of the patriarchs. Furthermore, each denies the other the right to the title.

Who is Israel? This question is vital to God's people. Its answer determines our basic theology. It sets the course for our interpretation of the Scriptures. It molds our opinion of God's plan for the earth.

Israel is an important, God-given title, therefore, the identity of the specific people it refers to must not be vague. The Israelites are God's chosen people. They are the ones destined to reign with God. For this reason, we need to know who they are.

For centuries the Church claimed the title of "Spiritual Israel." However, the rebirth of the State of Israel has caused an identity crisis within the Church. The return of the Jewish people to the Holy Land has caused many to question the age-old "Spiritual Israel—Physical Israel" titles. In addition, many question the relationship of the Church to Israel. Because of these changes, God's people now need to answer the age-old, decisive question: Who is Israel?

The most common responses to this crucial query are the following:

- Jacob, Whose Name Was Changed to Israel
- The Sons of Jacob—The Twelve Tribes
- The Land Given to the Twelve Tribes
- The Old Covenant People of God
- The Ten Tribes of the Northern Kingdom
- The Church
- The Jewish People
- The Present Jewish State

Israel—From Genesis to Revelation

In the Book of Genesis, we see God beginning to call forth the people of Israel. In the Book of Revelation, He invites His people to come into the New Jerusalem through the gates of the Twelve Tribes. Between Genesis and Revelation the name "Israel" is mentioned over 2,500 times. [1] It is mentioned so often because God is the God of Israel, and the Bible is a book about the people of Israel.

God declares that, ultimately, we will "name Israel's name with honor" (Isaiah 44:5). The *Theological Wordbook of the Old Testament* explains: "In the Restoration, Israel's title will be a truth, not a misnomer." [2]

God's children need to walk in this truth regarding Israel. They should not use the name as a "misnomer." If the Church is not Israel, she should not use Scriptures pertaining to Israel

3 ❧

when referring to herself. On the other hand, if the Church is Israel, a clear definition of the exact basis on which she is Israel must be developed. Likewise, if the Jewish people are Israel, then their right to the title must not be demeaned, nor should it be denied.

Through a careful examination of God's Word, [3] we can understand the mystery of Israel. First, however, we must gather all the pieces of information in the same way we would approach a jigsaw puzzle. Collectively, these pieces will reveal many much-needed truths—and they will provide a complete picture of Israel.

Let us begin our search by examining the meaning of the name itself. What is the definition of *Israel* ?

2
ISRAEL: THE MEANING OF THE NAME

&. The first mention of the name Israel was made by the angelic being who wrestled with Jacob. [1] During their unusual encounter, Jacob asked the angel to *bless* him. In response, the angel called him *Israel*.

What does the name mean? How is it a blessing? The answers to these questions provide a picture of—or at the very least, a standard for—the children of Israel.

Jacob's name is derived from the root word *a'kov*, meaning to grab the heel, to overreach, to supplant. [2] Jacob grabbed hold of his twin brother's heel during their birth and, fulfilling his name, ultimately acquired his first-born blessings by overreaching —taking matters into his own hands—supplanting.

God dealt with Jacob's nature during their confrontation in the wilderness. There Jacob met the Lord in repentance, for he "wrestled with the angel and prevailed; he wept and sought His favor" (Hosea 12:4). He confessed his name to be *Jacob*—the *supplanter*. After his repentant confession and after prevailing, God gave Jacob the name of Israel.

At Bethel, God appeared to Jacob and said: "You shall no longer be called Jacob, but Israel shall be your name" (Genesis 35:10). Hosea said of Jacob's encounter with God: "He found Him at Bethel, and there He spoke with us, even the Lord, the God of hosts; the Lord is His name" (Hosea 12:4-5).

God gave Jacob the name *Israel*, and at the same time, there *God* spoke with *us*. Through Jacob's blessing, God also spoke to the seed of Jacob: all who were in Jacob's loins when God called him Israel. He spoke to all who were to become Israel through Jacob. God spoke with *us* through Jacob.

His message is that through repentance, through perseverance, in the power and strength of the Almighty, Jacob was *given* the name Israel.

What does the name mean?

Yisrael comes from two words: *sarah*, a root word meaning to fight, to prevail, to have power as a prince; [3] and *el*, meaning strength, might, especially as in the Almighty. [4]

The *Gesenius Hebrew Lexicon* says *Israel* means "contender, soldier of God." [5] *Strong's Exhaustive Concordance* says it means one who "will rule as God." [6] *The New Brown-Briggs Lexicon* says that to be Israel is "to persist, to persevere." [7]

The Word tells us Jacob "*wrestled* with the angel" and that he had "*striven* with God." "Wrestled" and "striven" are both translated from the word *sarah*. In Jacob's encounter with the angelic being, he demonstrated an ability to stand as a prince. The *Theological Wordbook* explains: "Jacob's struggle was spiritual, in prayer, as well as physical. And in it the patriarch prevailed! Not that Jacob defeated God, but that he finally attained God's covenantal requirement of yielded submission....and he persisted in refusing to let the angel go until he had blessed him." [8]

For these reasons Jacob's name was changed to Israel, meaning...

A POWERFUL, PREVAILING PRINCE, A SOLDIER OF GOD; ONE WHO RULES WITH THE ALMIGHTY.

Where Is Israel To Prevail?

Jacob's call to be Israel was issued to him as a man. It was a call to prevail. To prevail means to be able, to be strong, to gain mastery, to triumph over, to be victorious. [9] That Israel is called to gain mastery in this world is evident because we know that in Heaven there is nothing to triumph over; all things are already in order in Heaven. Therefore, Israel's triumph, Israel's prevailing, must happen here—*in the earth.*

Israel must struggle against and gain mastery over *spiritual wickedness*: "For our struggle is not against flesh and blood, but against the rulers, against the powers, against the world forces of this darkness, against the spiritual forces of wickedness in the heavenly places" (Ephesians 6:12). God's people are directed to destroy "arguments and every pretension that sets itself up against the knowledge of God" (2 Corinthians 10:5, NIV).

And so it is for the heirs of Israel. [10] They are called to fight—as representatives of God—while on this earth. They are to fight a strong fight—and they are to prevail!

This understanding, however, must be tempered with the fact that, "flesh and blood cannot inherit the kingdom of God" (1 Corinthians 15:50). God is Spirit. [11] Therefore, to inherit His Kingdom, which is the Kingdom of Israel, [12] one must be a spiritual being.

The call to be Israel *begins here,* with people who are living in flesh-and-blood bodies. With God the seed is first sown in a natural body; then it is raised in a spiritual body (1 Corinthians 15:36-50). So it is for Israel: the call is twofold—it begins in the physical realm and it is culminated in the spiritual.

For this reason we must question the concept of separating Israel into physical and spiritual camps because...

ISRAELITES ARE PHYSICAL PEOPLE WHO ARE CALLED TO A SPIRIT-LED LIFE.

Jacob was called to be Israel—a powerful, prevailing prince—a warring prince who was to fight the spiritual battles of the Spirit God of Israel. Let us now examine *how* God said He would bless this one who was called to rule with Him.

3
THE BLESSING OF ISRAEL

ﷺ God's plan for blessing Israel is expressed in His multi-faceted blessing of Jacob. He said to him: "Your name is Jacob; you shall no longer be called Jacob, but Israel shall be your name." Thus He called him Israel. God also said to him, "I am God Almighty; be fruitful and multiply; a nation and a company of nations shall come from you, and kings shall come forth from you. And the land which I gave to Abraham and Isaac, I will give it to you, and I will give the land to your seed after you" (Genesis 35:10-12).

The first thing God did was to change Jacob's name to Israel. This signifies that it is God who determines when one is "a prince with God." He, not man, conveys the blessing.

Next, God commanded Jacob to be fruitful and to multiply. Also, He promised to give the land to Jacob, and to his seed after him. These two blessings given to the seed—fruitful multiplication and the land—are at the heart of all Old Covenant blessings.

Fruitful Multiplication

In Genesis 1:22, God said to the living creatures, "Be fruitful and multiply...on the earth." To man He said, "Be fruitful and multiply, and fill the earth" (Genesis 1:28). He commanded Noah and his sons to, "Be fruitful and multiply; populate the earth" (Genesis 9:7). God then declared to Abraham, "I will make you exceedingly fruitful, and I will make nations of you." He went on, "All the land which you see, I will give it to you and to your seed forever" (Genesis 17:6; 13:15). God said to Isaac, "I will multiply your seed as the stars of heaven, and will give your seed all these lands" (Genesis 26:4). Finally, God promised Jacob, "Be fruitful and multiply...and I will give the land to your seed after you" (Genesis 35:11-12).

"Fruitful" comes from a root word, *parah*, which means to bear fruit (literally or figuratively) and to cause to grow, to increase or make fruitful. [1] "Multiply" also comes from a root word, *rabah*. It means to cause to multiply, to increase, to make great, to excel exceeding(ly) and to be in authority. [2]

The heart of God's blessing to the seed of Israel is that she shall bear fruit, grow, be great in multiplying, excel exceedingly, and be in a position of authority by ruling with God.

The Enigmatic Seed

In addition, the blessings promised to Abraham, Isaac and Jacob are promised to *the seed*. In Hebrew, this word is *zera*. According to the *Theological Wordbook*: "The primary meaning comes from the realm of agriculture....Thus, the whole agricultural cycle is practically summed up in the word *zera*; from the act of sowing to the seed planted to the harvest taken....*Zera*[also] refers to semen....The word 'seed' is regularly used as *a collective noun in the singular* (never plural). This...is an important aspect of the promise doctrine, for Hebrew never uses the plural of this root to refer to 'posterity' or 'offspring'....Thus the word...is deliberately flexible enough to denote either one person who epitomizes the whole group (i.e. ...Christ), or the many persons in that whole line of natural and/or spiritual descendants." [3]

There are many possible meanings to be found in the blessing of the seed of Israel: *Zera* can be used in an agricultural sense (ie., sowing and reaping); it can mean the whole line of people; or it can mean Messiah.

The Eretz Is the Lord's

To Israel's *seed*, God promised the *eretz*, meaning land or earth. *Eretz* can mean a particular land, specifically the land of Canaan (later renamed Israel), or it can mean the whole earth. [4]

Thus there also are multiple meanings in the giving of the land. *Eretz* can indicate the particular land (Canaan) that was given to the twelve tribes (the descendants), as well as the land (earth) that *will* be given to the Messiah (the Seed). "Abraham and his offspring received the promise that he *would be* heir of the *world* " (Romans 4:13, NIV). Here God means the *cosmos*. [5]

Nonetheless, one day Messiah will return to a particular land: to His beloved chosen city, Jerusalem. [6] From there, as the King of Israel, [7] Jesus will rule the earth. [8]

But who are the Israelites who will rule with Him?

A Nation and a Company of Nations

God told Jacob, or Israel: "A nation and a company of nations shall come from you." Restated, God promised Jacob that he would be the father of both a *single* nation and a *congregation* of nations.

In Hebrew, God said a *goy* and a *kahal [of] goyim* would come from Jacob. The words *goy* (nation) or *goyim* (nations) also have several meanings. *Goy* has been used to describe Israel [9] and *goyim* to define political, ethnic or territorial groups (without ascribing a moral connotation). But most often, especially after the Israelites entered into Canaan and their covenant, *goyim* came to mean the non-covenant, non-believing, pagan, foreign nations surrounding Israel. It came to mean the Gentiles. [10]

The word *kahal* means a congregation or multitude of people gathered together, an assembly. [11] Since God is declaring who will come from Jacob, the *kahal [of] goyim* is a people from many nations, called together by God.

In Jacob's all-important blessing, God commanded him to be fruitful and to multiply. He said Israel would produce both a single nation and a congregation of nations. He also promised to give the land to the seed of Israel. Thus we have an outline of the blessing that was to come upon Jacob's heirs—the people of Israel.

In addition, God said Israel is His *first-born*. Therefore, to complete our profile of Israel, we now must define both the position and blessing of the first-born.

4
THE FIRST-BORN PROFILE

    🢨 God declared to the Pharaoh of Egypt: "Israel is My son, My first-born" (Exodus 4:22). In saying "Israel is My first-born," restated, God also was saying, *the first-born is Israel.* But who is this first-born Israel? Further, what does it mean to be the first-born? Are special privileges involved? Responsibilities?

The Evangelical Dictionary of Theology tells us: "Primogeniture, the exclusive right of inheritance belonging to the first-born, is traceable back to patriarchal times." [1]

Other textbooks declare: "The promises of God to the patriarchs were considered as attached to the line of the first-born" (Wycliffe Bible Encyclopedia). [2]

"All the first-born of Israel...belonged to Jehovah" (*Unger's Bible Dictionary*). [3]

The first-born son had "respect as leader among the brothers...and a double portion" (*Zondervan Pictorial Encyclopedia*). [4]

"He received the right to inherit family leadership and a double portion...(Genesis 43:33; Deuteronomy 21:17)" (*The New Harper's Bible Dictionary*). [5]

"Preferential status...sanctity, authority, sovereignty, responsibility, and right of succession accrued to the first-born...he became the next head of the family...and embodied the soul and character of the social group, becoming responsible for its continuance and welfare" (*Interpreter's Dictionary of the Bible*). [6]

"The first-born was the priest of the whole family" (*Unger's Bible Dictionary*). [7]

God, when instructing the father regarding the inheritance due the first-born, said: "He shall acknowledge the first-born...by giving him a double portion...to him belongs the *right* of the first-born" (Deuteronomy 21:17). The word *right* is translated from *mishpat*, meaning the ordinance of pre-eminence, the right to act as ruler, to dispense justice. [8]

From these descriptions we see that the first-born belonged to God. As the family priest, he was the embodiment of the soul and character of the social group. As head of the family, he was given authority and respect as leader among the brothers. As the first-born, he received preeminence, sovereignty and a double portion.

The Transferred Birthright

Despite all of this, "It was possible for the father to deprive the first-born of the right....Primogeniture was always considered but was not always decisive....The cases of transfer of birthright appear as exceptions which exemplify divine election" (*Wycliffe Bible Encyclopedia*). [9]

A careful study of God's Word reveals that the first-born birthright was often transferred: Ishmael was Abraham's first-born, but Isaac received sovereignty and preeminence. Jacob supplanted Esau and inherited the birthright. When God said, "Jacob I have loved, while Esau I have hated," [10] it was understood by all that Jacob, the second-born, was considered the heir.

The First-born Birthmarks

Since Jacob is the first to be called Israel, we must ask: To whom did he give his first-born blessing?

In Israel, the first-born is preeminent, a priest, a sovereign; he has a double portion. Therefore, if Israel has a first-born heir, he must meet all these specifications.

5
JACOB'S HEIR: WHO IS HE?

❧ Jacob's twelve sons—the Twelve Tribes of Israel—were born of his two wives, Leah and Rachel, and their handmaidens, Zilpah and Bilhah.

Leah bore Jacob's first-born son, Reuben. According to the right of primogeniture, the title of first-born belonged to him. However, the Chronicler tells us he was not the heir, but rather, "the birthright belonged to Joseph" (1 Chronicles 5:2).

Joseph was given Reuben's birthright. Why?

Reuben "defiled his father's bed"; for that reason, "his birthright was given to the sons of Joseph, the son of Israel; so that he is not enrolled in the genealogy according to the birthright" (1 Chronicles 5:1).

Reuben's birthright, or the title of first-born of Israel, was given both to Joseph and to his sons.

Joseph: A Type of Messiah

Joseph was Rachel's first-born son. He is often identified as a type of Messiah—a deliverer of the people of Israel.

In his two dreams, Joseph is seen as an erect sheaf, with his brothers as sheaves that bowed down to him; and as a star before whom his mother, father and brothers bowed. These dreams foretold his anointing—his position of leadership. They also caused his brothers to hate him, to strip him of his garments, and to sell him for twenty pieces of silver. [1]

Nonetheless, Joseph prevailed. Although he was sold into slavery, the evil actions taken against him by his brothers were turned around and ultimately, he became their deliverer.

While in Egypt, Joseph became the father of two sons, Manasseh and Ephraim. These two, along with Joseph, became the heirs of Israel. The intriguing story of how the blessing of Jacob passed from Joseph to the sons of Joseph unfolds in the forty-eighth chapter of Genesis.

When Jacob was nearing death, Joseph brought his sons to his father's bedside. "When it was told to Jacob, 'Behold, your son Joseph has come to you,' Israel collected his strength and sat up in the bed. Then Jacob said to Joseph, 'God Almighty appeared to me....and blessed me, and He said to me, 'Behold, I will make you fruitful and numerous, and I will make you a congregation of peoples, and will give this land to your seed after you for an everlasting possession'" (Genesis 48:2-4).

Because Joseph was the son of his beloved Rachel, "Israel loved Joseph more than all his sons" (Genesis 37:3). In addition, Jacob gave the first-born double portion to Joseph: "Israel said to Joseph....'I give you *one portion more* than your brothers'" (Genesis 48:21-22).

Jacob did this when he told Joseph: "And now your two sons, who were born to you in the land of Egypt before I came to you in Egypt, are mine; Ephraim and Manasseh shall be mine, as Reuben and Simeon are" (Genesis 48:5). Israel also said of them: "May my name live on in them, and the names of my fathers Abraham and Isaac" (Genesis 48:16).

Heirs by Adoption

Through this blessing, Jacob adopted Joseph's two sons. [2] His statement, "may my name live on in them," was possibly a recognized adoption formula. [3] According to the *ArtScroll Tanach Series*, [4] the Rabbis Rashbam and Rashi interpret the blessing to mean: "I accordingly pronounce you to be my first-born in this regard so you can receive the inheritance of two tribes." And, "They shall be counted among my other sons [not like my grandsons], each to have his own territory exactly like each of my other sons." [5]

But then Jacob carried his blessing one step further.

Ephraim, the Heir

Jacob said of Joseph's sons: " 'Bring them to me, please, that I may bless them'....And Joseph took them both, Ephraim with his right hand towards Israel's left, and Manasseh with his left hand towards Israel's right, and brought them close to him" (Genesis 48:9,13).

The position of each boy in relation to Israel's right hand is clarified because: "One traditionally blesses another by laying his hand on the person's head....The right hand is the preferred one for the performance of mitzvos [6] and, accordingly, has spiritual primacy" (*ArtScroll Tanach Series*). [7]

Genesis tells us, "Israel stretched out his right hand and laid it on the head of *Ephraim*, who was the younger, and his left hand on Manasseh's head, crossing his hands, although Manasseh was the first-born" (Genesis 48:14).

This was a deliberate act on Israel's part, through which "he put Ephraim before Manasseh" (Genesis 48:20).

In putting Ephraim before Manasseh, Israel was declaring that Ephraim was Joseph's heir. Jacob said, "Ephraim...shall be mine as Reuben" (Genesis 48:5). Or, in other words, "Ephraim shall be as *my* first-born."

Ezekiel confirms Ephraim as the heir when he says: "The stick of Joseph...is in the hand of Ephraim" (Ezekiel 37:19). God explained the purpose of these wooden sticks when He told Moses: "Speak to the sons of Israel, and get from them a rod for each father's household: twelve rods...You shall write each name on his rod...one rod for the head of each of their father's households" (Numbers 17:2-3). The *stick* Ezekiel speaks of is the "one *rod*." [8] The one who held the rod was the head of the house, and Ephraim holds Joseph's rod.

Why was Joseph's inheritance given to Ephraim rather than to Manasseh, the actual first-born? Why was the natural first-born again passed over in favor of another?

Divine Election

Abraham's first-born was Ishmael, but God elected Isaac, the second-born, as heir. Next, Isaac's first-born, Esau, was passed over in favor of Jacob. [9] Jacob, in turn, overlooked Reuben and chose Joseph, his eleventh son. Finally, Manasseh was passed over in favor of Ephraim.

Each of these elected first-born heirs have one thing in common: all were heirs of the blessing of Abraham through *adoption*!

JACOB'S HEIR: WHO IS HE?

Divine Intervention

Furthermore, with the exception of Ephraim (this exception will be explained later), each of the first-born heirs required divine intervention to bring them forth. We read of their mothers: "And Sarai was barren; she had no child." But God said, "I will bless her....and she shall be a mother of nations" (Genesis 11:30; 17:16). "And Isaac prayed to the Lord on behalf of his wife, because she was barren; and the Lord answered him and Rebekah his wife conceived" (Genesis 25:21). "But Rachel was barren....Then God remembered Rachel, and God gave heed to her and opened her womb" (Genesis 29:31; 30:22).

In each case, the womb of the mother of the first-born was opened by God. In each case, the first-born were not heirs by birthright; rather, they were heirs by adoption.

Through this, God demonstrates that He brings forth the first-born; they are determined according to His election. With Him, the giving of inheritance is not based "on man's desire or effort, but on God's mercy" (Romans 9:16, NIV).

Ephraim was divinely appointed as the first-born heir of Israel. But as the first-born, did he fulfill his call to become the head of the family—*the head who embodied the soul and character of Israel? Did Ephraim become a powerful, prevailing prince?*

6
EPHRAIM: A PROFILE

&. Ephraim's name, as an *individual*, is mentioned only fourteen times in the Scriptures. [1] We are told that he was born in Egypt, the son of Joseph and Asenath (daughter of Potiphera, priest of On). He was named Ephraim because God had made his father fruitful in the land of his affliction. Ultimately, he was brought before his grandfather and pronounced heir of Israel. The last mention of him is found in Genesis 50:23: "And Joseph saw the third generation of Ephraim's sons." After that, Ephraim disappears, leaving no record of his ever having passed his rich blessing on to another.

After Jacob blessed Ephraim, his descendants were considered as a single tribe. In addition, collectively, ten of the tribes became known as Ephraimites.

A House Divided

This came about because some time after the children of Israel entered into the land of Canaan, they divided into two houses: Judah and Ephraim.

This is a vital point in our understanding of Israel!

While all twelve tribes were considered descendants of Israel, the northern kingdom of Ephraim was primarily called Israel, and the southern kingdom was called Judah. [2]

The Scattered Ephraimites

The kingdom of Ephraim existed for approximately two hundred years (975-721 B.C.). [3] During that time the Scriptures intimate that there was an intermingling and intermarriage between the two kingdoms. [4] In all probability, each kingdom contained a representation of all the tribes.

We know the Northern Kingdom consisted of ten tribes (1 Kings 11:35). But because the Ephraimites often followed after the pagan customs of their Gentile neighbors, some of them joined the more godly people of Judah. [5] Those who joined Judah were thereafter considered subjects of the king of Judah: "But as for the sons of Israel who lived in the cities of Judah, Rehoboam [King of Judah] reigned over them" (1 Kings 12:17).

However, in spite of their intermingling, each house remained a separate kingdom. In fact, there was continual warfare between the two houses. This warring ceased only when Ephraim's northern foe, Assyria, carried the people of Ephraim away into captivity. [6]

In regard to the captivity of the Ephraimites, the *NIV Study Bible* states: "There is some evidence that Israel experienced its first deportations under Tiglath-Pileser III (745-727 B.C.), a cruelty repeated by Sargon II (722-705 B.C.) at the time of the fall of Samaria. The latter king's inscriptions boast of carrying away 27,290 inhabitants of the city as booty [7]....they were sent to Assyria, to Halah (Calah?), to Gozan on the Habor River, and apparently to the eastern frontiers of the empire (to the towns of the Medes, most probably somewhere in the vicinity of Ecbatana, the modern Hamadan)." [8]

After conquering a people, the Assyrians scattered them among other nations. Other conquered peoples were then moved into the newly subjugated land. [9] So was the case with the Ephraimites. They were scattered "in Halah, at the [River] Habor, at the River Gozan, and in the towns of Media" (2 Kings 17:6, TNKH. Also see 1 Chronicles 5:26). Next, "The king of Assyria brought men from Babylon...and settled them in the cities...in place of the sons of Israel" (2 Kings 17:24). These people ultimately became known as "Samaritans."

At the time the Ephraimites were taken captive they were functioning as a separate kingdom from Judah, having their own king (2 Kings 17:1-3). The locations they were taken to varied in distance from 250 to 350 miles north, northeast and northwest of Babylon—the place where Judah was later taken. It was 135 years later, or several generations, before the southern kingdom of Judah was taken captive. Furthermore, Judah was settled "*by* the river Chebar" (Ezekiel 1:1); but Ephraim was scattered "*beyond* the Euphrates River" (1 Kings 14:15).

What happened to the Ephraimites as a people? The *Encyclopaedia Judaica* says: "It is evident that as a rule they did not possess the status of slaves or of an oppressed population. The exiles were first settled in Mesopotamia as land tenants of the king...the craftsmen among them were employed in state enterprises. Eventually, some of the exiles

25 ❧

achieved economic and social status and even occupied high ranking positions in the Assyrian administration....The striking of roots in Mesopotamian society by a large part of the descendants of the Israelite exiles resulted in their eventual absorption into the foreign milieu." [10]

It is important to note:

These Ephraimites were Israelites and not Jews. During the time they lived in the land, they were never once called Jews. They were called Israelites. When they were scattered, they were Israelites who lived and worked in Assyria. They struck roots in Mesopotamian society. They were absorbed. They became foreigners. Gentiles.

The Judahites were taken captive more than a century and a quarter later. These were the Jews. It was the Jews who insisted upon maintaining a separate identity from the nations in which they lived. However, the Ephraimites wanted to be like the Gentiles. For that reason, God allowed them to become lost among the nations—to become Gentiles.

So went the fate of the Ephraimites.

From this brief history it would appear that the hallmark of the people of Ephraim is that *they are lost*—which is hardly a picture of a great congregation of people mightily blessed by God.

Where are the Ephraimites today?

The *Encyclopaedia Judaica* says the first century historian, *Josephus,* stated in his *Antiquities*: "The ten tribes are beyond the Euphrates till now, and are an immense multitude not to be estimated in numbers." [11] Alfred Edersheim, in his work, *The Life And Times Of Jesus The Messiah,* says: "The great mass of the ten tribes was in the days of Christ, as in our own, lost to the Hebrew nation." [12] Edersheim calls them, "Those wanderers of the ten tribes whose trackless footsteps seem as mysterious as their after-fate." [13] In Edersheim's study of Rabbinical thought regarding the lost tribes, he concludes: "As regards the ten tribes there is this truth underlying...that, as their persistent apostasy from the God of Israel and His worship had cut them off from His people, so the fulfillment of the Divine promises to them in the latter days would imply, as it were, a second birth to make them once more Israel." [14]

As the rabbis suggested, did the Ephraimites experience a "second birth"? Were the divine promises made to them fulfilled? Having become lost among the Gentile nations, did they once again become Israel?

Before we reach a conclusion, let us look at another facet of Ephraim's blessing.

7
THE FATHER OF A MULTITUDE

       ❧ Ephraim's forefather, Abraham, was told that he would be "the father of a multitude of nations" (Genesis 17:4). *Multitude*, or *hamon*, signifies more than a large number of people. It means a noise, a tumult, turbulence, wealth, multitude, company. [1] In using this word, God revealed to Abraham that he would be the father of a great multitude of peoples who would cause a tumultuous commotion in the earth! They would make a great noise (about God) throughout the world!

This promise of a great, earth-shaking congregation was given next to Isaac. The Lord said to him: "I will multiply your descendants as the stars of heaven" (Genesis 26:4). Here the word *multiply* is *rabah*, meaning to increase, to be full of, abundance, to become great, to be in authority. [2]

Next was added Rebekah's blessing: "Be thou the mother of

thousands of millions [or, *myriads*]" (Genesis 24:60, KJV). [3] Her husband, Isaac, then passed their blessing to Jacob: "May God...make you fruitful and multiply you, that you may become a congregation of peoples" (Genesis 28:3). God then confirmed this blessing by saying: "Thy seed shall be as the dust of the earth, and thou shalt spread abroad to the west, and to the east, and to the north, and to the south: and in thee and in thy seed shall all the families of the earth be blessed" (Genesis 28:14, KJV). To *spread out* is translated from *parats*, meaning to break forth, to increase. [4]

This blessing of increase was given next to Joseph. When preparing to bless him, Jacob said: "God Almighty...said unto me...I will make of thee a multitude of people" (Genesis 48:4, KJV). Here the word being translated *multitude* is *kahal*. Three times in the King James Version it is translated "multitude," eleven times "assembly," sixteen times "company" and sixty-six times "congregation." Clearly, the primary meaning is congregation—Congregation as in Church.

The Old Covenant "Church"

The Septuagint is a Greek translation of the Hebrew Old Covenant, completed 200 years before the birth of the Messiah. [5] In it, the Hebrew *kahal* is most often translated *ekklesia*, [6] the Greek word for Church. That means some 200 years *before* the birth of Jesus, Old Covenant Israel was called the "Church."

However, this does not mean "Greek westernized cultural Christianity." The godly call on Jacob's life cannot be limited to something as temporal as culture. [7]

THE FATHER OF A MULTITUDE

The Army Of Israel

Jacob's phenomenal blessing was independent of all earthly cultures. His name change carried implications far more important than cultural considerations. Jacob's God was *Yahweh Tze'va'ot*, [8] "The Lord of hosts, the God of the armies of Israel" (1 Samuel 17:45). Through Israel, the Lord of hosts was enlisting a powerful army, one that would engage in spiritual warfare. It would be an army called to overcome every principality or power raised against the God of Israel, a royal army called to rule forever with the Lord of Hosts.

The warriors in this army are not determined according to culture. Rather, holiness is the standard. "First-born rights" are not enough to qualify a person for this service. No. One is enlisted through election. One is chosen by the Lord of Hosts. In this army, He and He alone determines eligibility. [9]

Jacob, speaking of his earth-shaking army blessing, said of Manasseh and Ephraim: "May they be teeming multitudes upon the earth" (Genesis 48:16, TNKH). The *ArtScroll Series* translates it: "May they proliferate abundantly like fish." [10] The words being translated *multitude* are *va'yid'gu la'rov*. They mean, "may they multiply; may they grow into a multitude of fish." [11] This unusual term was used because they were to be a multitude of fish, caught by fishers of men.

Jacob used the pronoun *they*. May *they* grow into teeming, prolific multitudes. He said this because he knew it was Manasseh, and then Ephraim, who were to grow into the multitude of peoples promised to his forefather Abraham.

Jacob said, "[Manasseh]...shall become a people...However, his younger brother [Ephraim] shall be greater than he, and his descendants shall become a *multitude of nations*" (Genesis 48:19). The *ArtScroll Series* says the word used, *m'loh*, means a "fullness" and "connotes abundance...meaning: His seed will become the abundance of the nations....they will have to inhabit lands of other nations" [12]

Jacob said Ephraim's descendants would become a *m'loh [of] goyim,* or—*a fullness of Gentiles!*

Did Ephraim's descendants become a fullness of Gentiles, according to the blessing of Jacob?

For the answer, let us first take an allegorical look at Ephraim.

8
THE ALLEGORY

ᐧᐧ Within the Old Testament nation of Israel, the people of Ephraim were "a great company of nations." And, in the context of the multifaceted word *goy*, each tribe could be called a *nation*. Thus, they were a fulfillment of the promise to Ephraim. In fact, Joshua said: "The Lord gave to Israel the whole country which He had sworn to their fathers....Not one of the good things which the Lord had promised to the House of Israel was lacking. Everything was fulfilled" (Joshua 21:41-43, TNKH). [1]

King Solomon confirmed this fulfillment when he said, "Blessed be the Lord, who has given rest to His people Israel, according to all that He promised; not one word has failed of all His good promise, which He promised through Moses His servant" (1 Kings 8:56).

The *all* that was fulfilled was in reference to the

things promised through Moses. However, the blessings of Abraham, Isaac, Jacob, and Ephraim contained words having multiple meanings—*zera, eretz, goyim, kahal.* Thus New Covenant promises were also foretold in the blessing of "the seed of Israel."

The Apostle Paul teaches that Hagar and Sarah "may be taken figuratively" as representing two covenants (Galatians 4:24). In the same way, the theological truth of the two covenants is illustrated in Jacob's blessing of Manasseh and Ephraim. In it we can see a type, with Jacob as the Father, Joseph as the Messiah, Manasseh as Old Covenant Israel and Ephraim as New Covenant Israel.

As the deliverer of Israel, Joseph represents Jesus (Isaiah 59:20-21; Romans 11:26). Just as Joseph's double portion was given to Manasseh and Ephraim, so Jesus gives a double portion to all who will receive it. (Jesus said He was the Anointed One spoken of by Isaiah, and Isaiah said the Anointed One gives the double portion. See Luke 4:16-21; Isaiah 61:1-9.)

Manasseh portrays Old Covenant Israel in that the people of Manasseh were first a single tribe (nation) and later one of the many tribes (nations) that made up the Northern Kingdom of Ephraim. Likewise, the ethnic nation of Israel was first a single nation and is now one of the many nations God is gathering in His "Congregation of Nations"—The Church. [2]

Manasseh's name indicates a merciful forgetfulness—a consolation: [3] "Joseph named the first-born Manasseh. 'For,' he said, 'God has made me forget all my trouble and all my father's household' " (Genesis 41:51). To keep Joseph from becoming despondent over the loss of his family, God consoled him with a son, whose presence helped Joseph fulfill his God-given dreams. Likewise, the people of Old Covenant Israel were a consolation to God when He was grieving over the loss of His children after the fall of Adam. They were used to help establish God's Law, that He might begin the fulfillment of His dream—to save all who will turn to Him.

Ephraim is a type of New Covenant Israel. Joseph "named the second son Ephraim, 'For,' he said, 'God has made me fruitful in the land of my affliction' " (Genesis 41:52). According to *Strong's*, Ephraim means "double fruit." [4] The *Gesenius Hebrew Lexicon* says "double land." [5] Double land, double fruit. As the heir of Joseph, Ephraim was the son of the double portion, the son born in celebration of the fruitfulness of the deliverer while in a foreign land.

Messiah Jesus, like Joseph, was in a "foreign land." He left His native Heaven and came to a foreign world of sin. There, through His sacrifice, He gave birth to the sons who were to become a Congregation of Nations—and heirs of His double portion.

Egypt was the birthplace of both sons: "Now to Joseph in the land of Egypt were born Manasseh and Ephraim" (Genesis 46:20). Egypt is often seen as a picture of the world system, immorality and oppression of God's people. [6] Also, Manasseh and Ephraim were brought into the presence of the great patriarch Jacob by Joseph. In this way they were able to share in Joseph's double portion. Likewise, Jesus brings both children into the presence of the Father because both children need to be adopted: For, "all have sinned and fall short of the glory of God" (Romans 3:23). Regardless of our birth—Old Covenant, New Covenant, Jew, Gentile, bond or free—we *all* need to be adopted into the Father's family through Messiah the Deliverer. God "predestined us to adoption as sons *through* Jesus Christ." Through Him, we "have received the spirit of adoption as sons by which we cry out, 'Abba! Father!' " (Ephesians 1:5; Romans 8:15).

Through Jesus, those of Old Covenant and New are able to partake of His double portion—blessing in this life and in the life to come. This is in fulfillment of Jacob's prayer: "The God who has been my *shepherd* all my life to this day...bless the lads" (Genesis 48:15-16). Jacob asked the Good Shepherd, or Jesus (John 10:11), to bless both Old and New Covenant Israel.

Further, he said, "May my name live on in them, and the names of my fathers Abraham and Isaac" (Genesis 48:16). In fulfillment of this blessing their names do live on through Old and New Covenant Israel—in the pages of the Bible.

Finally, Manasseh is the older son, and elsewhere God said of older sons who did not receive the first-born portion: "The older shall *serve* the younger." And "your brother you shall *serve*" (Genesis 25:23; 27:40). Paul, in Romans 9 speaking of the older serving the younger, says it is not because either one has "done anything good or bad." But rather, it is "in order that God's purpose according to His choice might stand." For this reason it was said: "The older will serve the younger" (Romans 9:11-12).

Old Covenant Israel (Manasseh) served as an example in that they were used to show that God has a law—a standard for His Holiness. It is a high standard, one that cannot be met through our own righteousness. And because of Manasseh's example, the younger Congregation of Nations (Ephraim) learned of their need for Messiah's blood sacrifice.

Thus we see Manasseh as a type of Old Covenant Israel and Ephraim as a type of the Church.

Let us now return to Jacob's blessing to see *how* God planned to multiply the people of Israel.

9
THE PLAN

  God intended for the people of Israel to become myriads. He says He chose "the fewest of all peoples" (Deuteronomy 7:7). He swore He would make this few people "as numerous as the stars in the sky" (Exodus 32:13, NIV). Thus the *fewest* were to become *myriads*.

  Isaiah explained how God would do this. Speaking of a time when God would "honor Galilee of the Gentiles," he said: "Thou shalt *multiply* the nation....For to us a child is born, to us a son is given, and the government will be on His shoulders. And He will be called Wonderful Counselor, Mighty God, Everlasting Father, Prince of Peace. Of the increase of His government and peace there will be no end. He will reign on David's throne and over his kingdom, establishing and upholding it with justice and righteousness from that time on and forever. The zeal of the Lord Almighty will accomplish this" (Isaiah 9:3, NASB; and 6-7, NIV).

Israel was to be multiplied through the giving of a Son: The Seed of Abraham. God told Abraham and Jacob that through their seed, *"all* the families....*all* the nations of the earth shall be blessed" (Genesis 28:14; 22:18).

Paul says these "promises were spoken to Abraham and to his seed. He does not say, 'And to seeds,' as referring to many, but rather to one, 'And to your seed,' that is, Christ" (Galatians 3:16). The promise to Abraham was Jesus. Through Him would come the fullness of nations.

Through Jesus, multitudes would become heirs to the promise: "If you belong to Christ, then you are Abraham's offspring, heirs according to promise" (Galatians 3:29). Thus would Israel be multiplied.

One Blessing

Many try to separate the Church and Israel, claiming that the heirs of Abraham are not necessarily the heirs of Jacob. But these heirs of Abraham cannot be separated from Jacob because there is only one blessing.

God said to Isaac, "To you and to your seed...I will establish *the oath which I swore to your father Abraham*" (Genesis 26:3). Isaac said to Jacob, "May He [God] also give you *the blessing of Abraham*" (Genesis 28:4). "The covenant which He made with Abraham, and His oath to Isaac. He also confirmed it to Jacob for a statute, to Israel as an everlasting covenant" (1 Chronicles 16:16-17). Abraham "lived as an alien in the land of promise...with Isaac and Jacob, *fellow heirs of the same promise*" (Hebrews 11:9).

There is only one promise. Though the patriarchs dwelt in

the land of Israel, they realized that this in itself was not the fullness of that promise. While in the Land, they lived as aliens because they were "looking for the city which has foundations, whose architect and builder is God" (Hebrews 11:10). For that reason, we read: "*All* these died in faith, *without receiving the promises*, but having seen them and having welcomed them from a distance, and having confessed that they were strangers and exiles on the earth. For....they desire a better country, that is a heavenly one. Therefore God is not ashamed to be called their God; for he has prepared a city for them" (Hebrews 11:13-16).

The patriarchs did not receive the promises; they looked for a city—even as we do. Furthermore, we are told, "*only* together with *us* would they be made perfect" (Hebrews 11:40, NIV). Without *us*, the blessing promised the Patriarchs is incomplete.

That promise is made complete through First-born Israel.

10
GOD'S FIRST-BORN

 ▸ God calls three people His first-born. He says, "*Israel* is My first-born" and, "*Ephraim* is My first-born" (Exodus 4:22; Jeremiah 31:9). And Colossians tells us, "*His beloved Son....is the...first-born of all creation*" (Colossians 1:13-15).

In the previous Scriptures, God, speaking in the first person, identifies both Israel and Ephraim as *His* first-born. Yet we know that Jesus is God's First-born Son.

Since man is made in the image and likeness of God, [1] it seems reasonable that God, like man, has only one first-born. How then can we reconcile these Scriptures?

Could the answer be that the names Israel and Ephraim are names for Jesus?

We already recognize many names for Jesus. He is the

Bright Morning Star, the Son of David, Immanuel and the Lion of Judah, to list only a few of His many names. [2] Should we add to this list the names of Israel and Ephraim?

Jesus Is Israel

In the Scriptures, both Jacob and Jesus are called Israel. The Father and Jesus, speaking through Isaiah, said: "Listen to Me, O islands [the nations]....From the body of My mother He [God] named Me [Jesus]. And He has made My mouth like a sharp sword....And He [God] said to Me, '*You are My Servant, Israel*, In Whom I will show My glory'....And now says the Lord [God], who formed Me [Jesus] from the womb to be His Servant, to bring Jacob back to Him, in order that Israel might be gathered to Him...To raise up the tribes of Jacob and to restore the preserved ones of Israel; I [God] will also make You [Jesus] a light of the nations so that My salvation may reach to the end of the earth" (Isaiah 49:1-6).

Jesus is the fulfillment of Isaiah's prophecy in many ways. The nations were instructed to listen to "the One named from the body of His mother," and God named Jesus "Yeshua" (Hebrew for salvation), [3] before He was born (Matthew 1:21). Also, the One speaking has a mouth like a sharp sword. In Revelation 2:16, Jesus warns of the sword that is in His mouth. Furthermore, Isaiah says the Servant with the sword in His mouth is *Israel*.

God calls this One "My Servant Whom I have chosen" (Matthew 12:18). This Servant named Israel is not Jacob or his descendants. This Servant will *restore* the tribes of *Jacob*. He will *gather* the people of *Israel*.

Isaiah said this Israel is the One in Whom God will show His glory. When presented in the Temple as a first-born son,

Simeon said Jesus was: "A light of revelation to the Gentiles, and the *glory* of Thy people Israel" (Luke 2:32). Jesus is truly a *light* to the nations. As such, He is causing God's salvation to reach to the ends of the earth.

Finally, God, speaking of His love for *Israel*, says: "Out of Egypt I called My son" (Hosea 11:1). Matthew, speaking of *Jesus'* flight from Egypt, tells us: "So was *fulfilled* what the Lord had said through the prophet:'Out of Egypt I called *My son*' " (Matthew 2:15).

Jesus is Israel—the Israel through whom the people of Israel will be gathered to God.

Jesus Is the First-born

God promised David: "I will establish your *seed forever*, and build up your throne to all generations." God then said of this promised seed: "His throne...shall be established forever like the moon" (Psalms 89:3-4,36-37).

David knew this *seed* would come after he died, [4] because God explained to David: "When your days are *complete* and you *lie down* with your fathers, I will raise up your seed after you...I will establish *his* kingdom. He shall build a house for My name, and I will establish the throne of *his* kingdom *forever*. I will be a father to him and he will be a son to Me....[and, thus] your house and your Kingdom shall endure before Me forever; your throne shall be established forever" (2 Samuel 7:12-16). [5]

God also declared this promised Son of David to be His First-born. He said of Him: "He will cry to Me, 'Thou art my Father, My God, and the rock of my salvation.' I also shall make him *My first-born*, The highest of the Kings of the earth. My lovingkindness I will keep for him forever, and My covenant shall be confirmed to him. So I will establish his seed forever, and his throne as the days of heaven" (Psalms 89:26-29).

Jesus has fulfilled this First-born prophecy. As the Son of God, He cried to His Father from the cross. He was then resurrected, as the First-born from the dead, the Highest of the Kings of the earth. Through Him, Israel's New Covenant and David's eternal throne were established. [6]

Jesus Is Ephraim

Before seeing in greater detail how Jesus also is Ephraim the First-born, we must lay more foundation. For now, let us note that the Scriptures identify both God *and* Ephraim as the *maoz. Maoz* means a place of safety, a very present help, a refuge, a fortress. [7]

The Word says, "*God* is my [*maoz*] strong fortress" (2 Samuel 22:33). King David said of God: "*Thou* art my [*maoz*] strength"; the "God [Who] is our refuge and strength, a very present help in trouble" (Psalm 31:4; 46:1). While the Word declares God to be the *maoz*, it also says, "God hath spoken in his holiness....Ephraim also is the strength [*maoz*] of mine head" (Psalm 108:7-8, KJV).

God and Ephraim both are the *maoz*. Together, they are the ever-present strength, the very-present refuge Who offers salvation.

The blessing of Ephraim—that of becoming *the fullness of nations*—is truly fulfilled only through Jesus because it is "the Father's good pleasure for *all the fullness* to dwell in Him" (Colossians 1:19).

Let us now see how that is being fulfilled.

11
THE BRETHREN OF THE FIRST-BORN

    ❧ God swore regarding His First-born: "My covenant shall be confirmed to him. So I will establish *his seed forever*" (Psalm 89:28-29). In fulfillment of this promise, Jesus is being given myriads of children who will live eternally.

He has "given birth" to myriads of children for whom He travailed in labor, a painful, hard labor on the Tree, [1] a labor that was to give birth to a new creation; a labor so painful He died from it. Jesus died to give birth to the sons of righteousness.

Through faith in Jesus, these children become sons of God: to "as many as received Him, to them He gave the right to become children of God, even to those who believe in His name" (John 1:12). When one believes in the Name of Jesus, God's "seed abides in him...because he is *born of God*" (1 John 3:9). These children "have been born again not of seed which is perishable but imperishable, that is, through the living and abiding word of God" (1 Peter 1:23).

These are the eternal descendants promised to the First-born—they have His imperishable seed abiding in them—they are "the Israel of God" (Galatians 6:16).

However, once these children are born anew, God desires to conform them to the image of His Son: "For whom He foreknew, He also predestined to become conformed to the image of His Son, that He might be the first-born among many brethren" (Romans 8:29).

The First-born Double Portion

These brethren share in the double portion of the First-born, which is given by the Lord's *Anointed*. [2] Jesus declared Himself to be that Anointed One when standing in the synagogue. There He read from Isaiah: "The Spirit of the Lord is upon Me, because He anointed Me to preach the gospel...to proclaim release to the captives...to set free those who are downtrodden" (Luke 4:17-21). Isaiah said this same Anointed One would "comfort all who mourn...giving them...the oil of gladness....the mantle of praise....So they will be called....the priests of the Lord....[And then,] instead of your shame you will have a *double portion*....they will shout for joy over their portion....they will possess a *double portion* in their land, everlasting joy will be theirs" (Isaiah 61:2-7).

The double portion is for all who receive Messiah's good news. Those who mourn over their sins are anointed with the oil of His forgiveness. Then, instead of shame, they have a double blessing.

Moses also spoke of the double portion. He said: "The Lord has given you the Sabbath; that is why on the sixth day he gives you bread for two days" (Exodus 16:29, NIV). The children of

Israel, having their double portion, could rest on the Sabbath. Likewise, Hebrews 4:9 says: "There remains, then, a Sabbath-rest for the people of God" (NIV). Those who receive the good news of Messiah have the bread of life in this life (the sixth day), and they have life in the world to come. They rest in Messiah's Sabbath—true children of the double portion.

The Congregation of the First-born

These children also are called "to the general assembly and *church of the first-born* who are enrolled in heaven...to Jesus, the mediator of a new covenant" (Hebrews 12:23-24).

In this Scripture the Greek word translated *first-born* does not refer to the Messiah; rather, it is used in the plural. Jay P. Green, in *The Interlinear Bible*, translates the verse: We have come to "a church of *first-born ones." The New International Version Bible* translates it in the plural: "To the church of the firstborn whose *names* are written in heaven." They are *first-born ones* whose *names* are written in Heaven because they have become *one* with the First-born—Jesus.

He is the "head of the body, the church; he is the beginning and the first-born from among the dead, so that in everything he might have the *supremacy"* (Colossians 1:18, NIV).

In Israel, Jesus has the first-born supremacy and the double portion. He is the High Priest and the King of kings. He alone can fulfill all the requirements to be Jacob's heir. He is both Israel the First-born and Ephraim the First-born.

The titles are His, because He is the epitome of the Powerful, Prevailing Prince of Israel—the only One who is truly capable of ruling with God.

Physical or Spiritual Brothers?

Jesus is Israel. Therefore, His brethren, those of the Church, are the brethren of Israel. But on what basis are they Israel?

Thus far we have dealt primarily with allegory, with types and shadows. But does the Church hold a greater claim to the title of Israel? Is there more to Jacob's blessing than allegory? Did Jacob literally mean the Ephraimites would *physically* become a fullness of Gentiles?

The Apostle Paul made it clear that up until his time the fullness of Gentiles was a mystery. He said: "By revelation there was made known to me the *mystery*...to be specific, that the Gentiles are fellow heirs and fellow members...fellow partakers of the promise" (Ephesians 3:3,6).

Somehow, mysteriously, in Israel the Gentiles are fellow heirs.

Are the Gentiles Paul speaks of somehow also physically the fullness of nations promised to Ephraim?

Is this the mystery?

12
BECOMING PHYSICAL ISRAEL

    🙰 The Church is a gathering of physical people who seek to have their spirits master their souls and bodies. But are they *physical* Israelites? Could they possibly be a *natural* Israel by birth?

In answering these questions, we must willingly accept what the Scriptures say—not what man says—about how a person becomes part of natural Israel. We must receive our answers from the Word of God—not from tradition.

God wanted the Israelites to be an example of His blessings. In this way, they would provoke those around them to jealousy, thus drawing others to them. For this reason, God gave Israel laws, or "loving instructions." Their adherence to these instructions regarding diet, cleanliness, civil law and worship would improve their standard of living. God told them: "You shall therefore keep every commandment...*so that you may be strong* " (Deuteronomy 11:8).

While God intended that the people of Israel be set apart for Himself—and absolutely did not want them to be converted to Gentile ways—He did desire to have others converted to *their* ways. Therefore, He made definite provisions for all who would join His covenant people. He gave three conditions which, when met, opened wide the door of commonwealth in Israel.

He said: "If a stranger who dwells with you would offer the passover to the Lord, all his males must be circumcised; then he shall be admitted to offer it; he shall then be as a citizen of the country" (Exodus 12:48, TNKH).

God made it clear that one joined the people of Israel by observing *circumcision, Passover* and *sojourning.* Having met these requirements, they were citizens—*native Israelites.* God said, "If an alien sojourns among you and observes the Passover to the Lord, according to the statute of the Passover and according to its ordinance, so he shall do; you shall have one statute, both for the alien and for the native of the land" (Numbers 9:14). "There shall be one law for the citizen and for the stranger who dwells among you" (Exodus 12:49, TNKH). "The alien living with you must be treated as one of your native-born. Love him as yourself, for you were aliens in Egypt" (Leviticus 19:34, NIV).

Not making a difference between native and sojourner was so important to God that He restated it on more than twenty-five occasions. [1]

Furthermore, this rule was declared a perpetual statute in Israel: "The community is to have the same rules for you and for the alien living among you; *this is a lasting ordinance for the generations to come.* You and the alien shall be the same before the Lord: The same laws and regulations will apply both to you and to the alien living among you" (Numbers 15:15-16, NIV).

Let Not!

In addition, God instructed those who joined the people of Israel as to how they were to regard themselves: "Let not the foreigner who has joined himself to the Lord say, 'The Lord will surely separate me from His people' " (Isaiah 56:3).

Let not the foreigner say he is separate from God's people Israel! Rather, God said: The " 'foreigners who bind themselves to the Lord to serve him, to love the name of the Lord, and to worship him, all who keep the Sabbath without desecrating it and who hold fast to my covenant—these I will bring to my holy mountain and give them joy in my house of prayer. Their burnt offerings and sacrifices will be accepted on my altar; for My house will be called a house of prayer for all the nations.' The Sovereign Lord declares—he who gathers the exiles of Israel: '*I will gather still others to them* besides those already gathered' " (Isaiah 56:6-8, NIV).

In Israel, there was one law for the native and the sojourner. The Gentiles who sojourned with Israel, those who were circumcised and observed the Passover, were specifically instructed not to see themselves as separate from Israel! Furthermore, God declared these to be lasting ordinances for all generations to come!

Let us now see how these requirements are fulfilled in the New Covenant.

13
NEW COVENANT ISRAEL

* Moses spoke of heart circumcision when he said: "The Lord your God will circumcise your heart and the heart of your descendants...that you may live" (Deuteronomy 30:6). Later, God more clearly defined this coming New Covenant of the heart. He said, " 'This is the covenant which I will make with the house of Israel after those days,' declares the Lord, 'I will put My law within them, and on their heart I will write it; and I will be their God, and they shall be My people'" (Jeremiah 31:33).

God said He would make a New Covenant with *the house of Israel.* This promise was not made to the nations. Rather, it was made to Israel. To partake of this covenant, one *joined* the people of Israel.

God further promised to raise up a prophet who would institute this Covenant. Moses said of Him: "The Lord your

God will raise up for you a prophet like me from among your own brothers. *You must listen to him*" (Deuteronomy 18:15, NIV). God said, "I will put My words in his mouth and he will speak to them all that I command him; and if anybody fails to heed the words he speaks in My name, I Myself will call him to account" (Deuteronomy 18:18-19, TNKH).

That Prophet is Jesus—the One who "has been found worthy of greater honor than Moses" (Hebrews 3:3, NIV). That means God commanded Israel to listen to Jesus. And Jesus commanded the people of *Israel* to observe the *New Covenant Passover!*

New Covenant Passover

Jesus told Peter and John: "Go and make preparations for us to eat the Passover" (Luke 22:8, NIV). While reclining at the table, Jesus said, "I have earnestly desired to eat this Passover with you before I suffer" (Luke 22:15).

Jesus desired to eat *this* particular Passover because in *its* observance, He instituted the New Covenant Passover.

With whom was Jesus establishing the New Covenant Passover?

Twelve sons of Israel. Twelve sons of Israel observed the first Passover of New Covenant Israel!

In it, Jesus taught the people: " 'This is My body which is given for you; do this in remembrance of Me.' And in the same way He took the cup after they had eaten, saying, 'This cup which is poured out for you is the new covenant in My blood' " (Luke 22:19-20).

That Passover was the last of the Old Covenant Passovers and the first of the New Covenant Passovers. No longer is the central focus to be the blood of a substitute animal; now it is the Blood of the Son of God. [1]

Through His death on the Tree, Jesus became our Passover Lamb (1 Peter 1:19). For that reason it is said: "Christ our Passover [Lamb] has been sacrificed" (1 Corinthians 5:7, TAB).

The Apostle Paul further explained: "As often as you eat this bread and drink the cup, you proclaim the Lord's death until He comes" (1 Corinthians 11:26).

We want to proclaim Jesus' death because through it we declare we belong to New Covenant Israel (Ephesians 2:13-14) and not to the people of the world (Colossians 1:20). Therefore, the angel of *the second death* will *pass over* us in the final judgment (Luke 22:16; Romans 5:9; Ephesians 1:7-14). He will pass over because we are sanctified by the Blood of the New Covenant Passover Lamb (Hebrews 13:11-12). Through it we have an eternal sacrifice for our sins (Hebrews 9:12,15,26; 13:20). Thus we are the eternal Israel of God (Galatians 6:16).

New Covenant Circumcision

The law regulating the Passover celebration also stated that "no uncircumcised person shall eat of it" (Exodus 12:48, TAB). Jesus revealed how His people meet this condition. He said: "Behold, I stand at the door and knock; if anyone hears My voice and opens the door, I will come in to him" (Revelation 3:20).

Jesus spoke of the door of the heart because in the New Covenant, "Circumcision is that which is of the heart, by the Spirit, not by the letter; and his praise is not from men, but from God" (Romans 2:29).

When the door of the heart is opened, Jesus comes in to circumcise it. We are then "circumcised with a circumcision made without hands, in the removal of the body of the flesh by the circumcision of Christ; having been buried with Him in baptism" (Colossians 2:11-12). Through this circumcision, we become "the true circumcision, who worship in the Spirit of God and glory in Christ Jesus and put no confidence in the flesh" (Philippians 3:3).

When one opens the door of his heart, Jesus says: "I will come in to him, and will dine with him, and he with Me" (Revelation 3:20). We dine with Jesus at His communion table; there we partake of the Passover of New Covenant Israel. In this way, New Covenant Israel fulfills the requirements for circumcision and Passover.

New Covenant Sojourning

An additional requirement for inclusion in the common-wealth of Israel was to *sojourn* with the people. However, only if the early Believers remained physical Israelites could others fulfill this requirement with them. Therefore we must ask: Did the early Believers remain physical Israelites? Would the so-journing requirement be fulfilled by joining with them?

We know the apostles were native-born, natural Israelites. In addition, multiplied thousands of members during the early years of the Church were Israelites. [2] These natural Israelites heeded the words of the prophet foretold by Moses. They obeyed the commands of Jesus. God said, "Anyone who does *not* listen to him will be completely cut off from among his people" (Acts 3:23, NIV). Surely God did not *reward* the *obedience* of the first Believers and their descendants by cutting them off from being Israel!

To be part of Israel is to partake of a *blessing*—it is to reign with God. Therefore, we must conclude that through their obed-ience, the early Believers remained *natural* children of Israel.

In addition, these people surely had thousands upon thousands of natural Israelite children, who remained in the Church. *Dr. Bill Hamon*, in his book, *The Eternal Church*, says: "By the close of the first century there were families which for three generations had been Christian. The grandchildren of Peter and John could have been active ministers in the Church by this date." [3]

Since the early Church was made up of natural Israelites and since their descendants were natural blood-line relatives, what of those from the nations—those who sojourned with the early Church? Did they not fulfill God's sojourning requirement by becoming one with these natural Israelites?

If these converts also became circumcised of heart and partook of the New Covenant Passover along with natural Israel, did they not meet *all* of God's requirements to *physically become* part of Israel? Should they not be considered—according to the Scriptures—as fully qualified members of the House of Israel?

God decreed that once a sojourner fulfilled His requirements, he was no longer a sojourner, but a full citizen—an Israelite. Therefore, according to the Word of God, those who sojourned with them also were a naturalized Israel—a naturalized Israel abiding by a spiritual covenant.

14
THE OLIVE TREE

❧ Speaking to the houses of Israel and Judah, Jeremiah said: "The Lord called your name, 'a green olive tree' " (Jeremiah 11:16).

Those who enter into Israel's New Covenant are grafted into "the rich root of the olive tree" (Romans 11:17).

In the olive tree of Israel, every branch receives its support from Jesus, who is the Root of David. [1] In this tree there are natural branches stemming from branches that have remained from the beginning. Around its base, there are branches that have been broken off for unbelief. In addition, this tree has wild olive branches that have been grafted in. However, once grafted into Jesus, there is no longer a distinction between wild and natural branches. All are part of the olive tree of Israel. [2]

In a natural tree, once branches are grafted in, all new shoots born of the former wild branches are natural branches.

The same is true with God's people. Once grafted into the Root of David *they no longer give birth to pagan Gentiles! Rather, they produce natural Israelites!*

However, in fear and trembling every branch must remember: Branches are "broken off for unbelief"! Every branch "stands only by faith"! (Romans 11:20).

Former Gentiles

The Apostle Paul, when instructing the Gentiles who were being grafted in, said: "Remember that *formerly* you who are Gentiles by birth...you *were*...excluded from citizenship in Israel and foreigners to the covenants of the promise, without hope and without God in the world. But now in Christ Jesus you who once were far away have been brought near through the blood of Christ. For he himself is our peace, who made the two one" (Ephesians 2:11-14, NIV).

To be a *Gentile* means to be a *heathen.* [3] *Formerly* means *in time past.* [4] In other words, you were heathens, having foreign gods and thus being foreign to the God of Israel. [5] However, now you have been brought *near* to the covenants of Israel. Exactly how near is revealed through another use of the same Greek word: [6] "The word is *near* you; it is in your mouth and in your *heart*" (Romans 10:8, NIV). God brought the Gentiles as near as the heart—the very center of life! [7]

Paul said, "You are no longer outsiders—exiles, migrants and aliens, [8] excluded from the rights of citizens." Now you "share citizenship with...God's own people" (Ephesians 2:19, TAB).

Ruling Saints

These Israelites share citizenship with "the *saints* [who] will judge the world" (1 Corinthians 6:2). These saints are

Israelites, for God told Israel: "You may not put a foreigner over yourselves who is not your countryman" (Deuteronomy 17:15). To judge another is to *rule* over him; thus the saints who will judge are Israel—the powerful, prevailing prince who rules with God.

Daniel said, "The Ancient of Days came and...the *saints* of the Most High...possessed the Kingdom" (Daniel 7:22, NIV). Jesus told His followers: "Your Father has been pleased to give *you* the Kingdom" (Luke 12:32, NIV). These saints of Israel who are given the Kingdom are also called...

The Chosen People

God called the people of Israel to be "a holy people to the Lord...chosen...to be a people for His special treasure" (Deuteronomy 14:2). The Israelites are a chosen, precious treasure—a position that is reaffirmed to New Covenant Israel. God says they are "chosen by God and precious to Him" (1 Peter 2:4, NIV).

The Royal Priesthood

The chosen people of Israel were also called to be "a kingdom of priests and a holy nation." (Exodus 19:6, KJV). This would come about because the Lord swore in regard to His priests: "I will make...the Levites who minister before me as countless as the stars of the sky and as measureless as the sand on the seashore" (Jeremiah 33:22, NIV).

These innumerable priests were "purchased, bought with a price," by the Messiah—who "gave Himself for us, that He might redeem...for Himself a people for His own possession" (1 Corinthians 6:20; 7:23; Titus 2:14). With His blood, Jesus purchased men for God from every tribe and language and people and nation. [9] And He made them to be "a kingdom and priests to serve our God, and they will reign on the earth" (Revelation 5:9-10, NIV).

Those Israelites who take part in God's first resurrection are told: "Blessed and holy is the one who has a part in the first resurrection; over these the second death has no power, but they will be priests of God and of Christ and will reign with Him for a thousand years" (Revelation 20:6).

God speaks of a people who will be co-rulers with His Messiah. But *physically*, who makes up this holy nation that is destined to reign with God?

The Apostle Peter gives the answer. He says he wrote to the "aliens"—to those who "once were not a people" (1 Peter 1:1; 2:10). To those people he said: "But *you* are a chosen race, a royal priesthood, a holy nation, a people for God's own possession" (1 Peter 2:9).

The *NIV Study Bible* says of the "aliens" who "once were not a people": "In Hosea it is Israel who is not God's people; in Romans it is the Gentiles to whom Paul applies Hosea's words; in 1 Peter the words are applied to both." [10]

These words are applied to *both*. Could they be one and the same people?

15
LO-AMMI

ই৯ *Lo-Ammi. You are not My people.*

God spoke these words to the Northern Kingdom. [1] With them, He decreed an end to the kingdom of the house of Israel. However, it was the end of the *kingdom*—not the end of the *people*. In His eyes, the people of Ephraim continue to exist, even though they no longer are a recognizable kingdom.

We see this in that more than 100 years after the kingdom ended, [2] God said through Jeremiah: " 'Is Ephraim My dear son? Is he a delightful child? Indeed, as often as I have spoken against him, I certainly still remember him; therefore My heart yearns for him; I will surely have mercy on him,' declares the Lord" (Jeremiah 31:20).

God planned *eventually* to have mercy on the people of Ephraim. But first, they had a lesson to learn. Therefore, prior to scattering them, God used Hosea, and his marriage and children, to portray both the condition of the Ephraimites and God's ultimate plan for them.

God said to Hosea, "Go, take to yourself a wife of harlotry, and have children of harlotry; for the land commits flagrant harlotry, forsaking the Lord" (Hosea 1:2).

The lust of the Ephraimites for the things of the Gentiles angered God. The punishments for their actions were represented in the names given to the children of Hosea. Nonetheless, God promised one day these punishments would be turned away and again the names of the children would be used—this time to illustrate God's blessings. [3]

When Hosea's wife, Gomer, bore him a son, God said of him: "Name him Jezreel; for yet a little while...and I will put an end to the kingdom of the house of Israel" (Hosea 1:4). *Jezreel* comes from two words: *zera* (seed), used in the agricultural sense of to sow or to scatter, and *El*, one of the names of God. Together they mean *God will scatter, God will sow.* [4] Since the people had sown much spiritual harlotry, God declared He would *scatter their seed* (descendants) in the land of their enemies. [5]

When Hosea's wife conceived a second time, she bore him a daughter. God told Hosea to "Call her name Loruhamah, or Not-pitied, for I will no more have loving-kindness, pity and mercy for the house of Israel, that I should in any way pardon them" (Hosea 1:6, TAB). Israel's sins of harlotry were such that punishment had to be meted out.

This impending punishment was revealed in the name of yet another son. God said of him: "Name him Lo-Ammi, for you are not My people and I am not your God" (Hosea 1:9).

The descendants of Ephraim were destined to become *Lo-Ammi. Not My People.*

A Promised Blessing

However, to these *same* people, God said: "Yet the number of the sons of Israel will be like the sand of the sea, which cannot be measured or numbered; and it will come about that, in the place where it is said to them, 'You are not My people,' it will be said to them, 'You are the sons of the living God' " (Hosea 1:10). [6]

Because of their idolatry, for a time the Ephraimites would be "not My people." Then, one day, they would be restored —to become *the sons of the living God*"!

Scattered Seed

Before this restoration could take place, God had said, "Israel will certainly go into exile, away from their native land" (Amos 7:11, NIV). "I will shake the house of Israel [like seed] among *all* the nations" (Amos 9:9, NIV). "They will not remain in the Lord's land, but Ephraim will return to Egypt" (Hosea 9:3). "God will cast them away because they have not listened to Him; and they will be wanderers among the nations" (Hosea 9:17). "Thus shall the sons of Israel eat their bread unclean among the nations where I shall banish them" (Ezekiel 4:13).

Scattered Ephraim would return to Egypt—to worldliness. God made it clear their downfall came because "Ephraim mixes himself with the nations." As a result, "Ephraim has become a cake not turned. Strangers devour his strength, yet he does not know it" (Hosea 7:8-9).

Ephraim mixed with pagan Gentiles. They became a cake not turned—or half-baked. They were like a pancake cooked on one side, having a partial relationship with the fire of God's

Spirit, but the other side was raw—pagan. Foreigners sapped them of their strength. They entertained foreign gods and doctrines, losing the strength to be the powerful, prevailing prince Israel was called to be. [7]

God warned Israel "not to be counted among the nations" (Numbers 23:9). Rather, they were to be a holy people, set apart, belonging solely to Him.

Because Ephraim wanted to be like the Gentiles around them, God gave them over to their desire. He declared: "Israel is swallowed up; they are now among the nations like a vessel in which no one delights" (Hosea 8:8).

Gentile Israel

Swallowed is translated from the Hebrew *bala*, meaning to make away with by swallowing, to devour, to be at an end, to swallow down. [8] That is what happened to the people of Ephraim. They were swallowed up among the nations. They became "not my people." Gentiles.

To this day the Ephraimites remain unidentifiable as a nation. In fact, being unidentifiable is their hallmark. As a people they were lost among every tribe, tongue, people and nation.

The people of Judah, unlike the people of Ephraim, have maintained their identity. [9] For 2,000 years, because of persecution, Judah has repeatedly either had to, or possibly wanted to, hide their identity. But, even in their dispersion, they have always been known as Jews.

These people, when they returned from Babylon to Jerusalem, returned as the people of Judah. Though a representation of each of the twelve tribes may have returned with them, all agree, not all the Ephraimites returned—nor has there ever been a formal return of the northern tribes to reestablish their kingdom. Furthermore, those of Ephraim who joined Judah were thereafter known as Judahites. While they may have known from which tribe they were descended, they were no longer known as Ephraimites.

The Ephraimites went the same way as a piece of meat when it is swallowed by a man—it literally becomes part of his flesh. And so the people of Ephraim were swallowed up by the nations, never again to be known by mankind as the people of Ephraim.

Jezreel

Nonetheless, God made an incredible promise to the Ephraimites: He said there would come a day when Ephraim "will respond to Jezreel" (Hosea 2:22).

God put an end to their kingdom by *scattering* them among the nations. However, in its second stage, Jezreel indicates a *sprouting*, a result of God's sowing. [10] In the first Jezreel, the Ephraimites were like seed that had to die. But in the second Jezreel, God says they will sprout as an abundant harvest in His land. God said: "I will sow her for Myself in the land. I will also have compassion on her who had not obtained compassion, and I will say to those who were not My people, 'You are My people!' and they will say, 'Thou art My God!' " (Hosea 2:23).

God promised a day of harvest—a time of restoration for the Ephraimites. Though scattered among the nations, God Himself knows where they went—and He knows where their descendants are today. Therefore, He could make, and keep, a promise to gather the scattered.

First Fruits—Vessels of Mercy

God does not consider the descendants of Ephraim nor Judah as being lost to Himself. For that reason He prompted the Apostle James to address his letter "to the twelve tribes *scattered among the nations.*" To them, James said: "He chose to give *us* birth through the word of truth, that *we* might be a kind of *first fruits* of all he created" (James 1:1,18, NIV). God had James write to the *first fruits of the scattered seed of Israel.*

Hosea said, "Israel is...among the nations...a *vessel* in which no one delights" (Hosea 8:8). Yet, God promised "compassion on her who had not obtained compassion" (Hosea 2:23). God speaks of His tenderness for those scattered vessels when He calls them His "vessels of mercy, which He prepared beforehand for glory" (Romans 9:23).

Paul says these vessels of mercy are "even *us,* whom He also called, not from among Jews only, but *also from among Gentiles.* As He says also in Hosea, "I will call those who were not My people, 'My people,' and her who was not beloved, 'Beloved,' and it shall be that in the place where it was said to them, 'You are not my people,' there they shall be called 'Sons of the living God' " (Romans 9:24-26).

Those of Ephraim who were scattered like seed among the nations, those who were not His people, vessels in whom no one took delight—were destined one day to become vessels of mercy, first fruits, sons of the Living God.

16
THE LOST SHEEP OF ISRAEL

• Micaiah, the prophet, told the king of Ephraim: "I saw all Israel, scattered on the mountains, like sheep which have no shepherd" (1 Kings 22:17). While there was an immediate battle at hand that would scatter the Ephraimites, in addition, a day would come when they would be scattered throughout the nations. [1]

Though God called the Ephraimites "faithless Israel," He also spoke of a day of deliverance, a day when the descendants of these faithless sheep would *return* in repentance.

God commanded Jeremiah: "Go, and proclaim these words toward the north [where the ten tribes have been taken as captives] and say, 'Return, faithless Israel' " (Jeremiah 3:12, TAB).

God's plan for their return was explained by Micah: "But as for you, Bethlehem Ephrathah...from you One will go forth for

Me to be ruler in Israel. His goings forth are from long ago, from the days of eternity." God stated that *after* the One from Bethlehem went forth: "Then the remainder of His brethren will return to the sons of Israel. And He will arise and shepherd His flock....And this One will be our peace"(Micah 5:2-5). ²
Through the Shepherd, the scattered Israelites would *return*, or be counted once again, among the sons of Israel.

Confirming this plan, Isaiah said: "Therefore the redeemed of the Lord shall *return*, and come with singing unto Zion" (Isaiah 51:11, KJV). Only if the redeemed were once in Israel (in the loins of their forefathers), could they *return*. God is speaking of the descendants of the Israelites, returning in repentance to the Shepherd of Israel.

The Shepherd God

God promised that "He who scattered Israel will gather him and keep him as a shepherd keeps his flock" (Jeremiah 31:10) and "For thus says the Lord God, 'Behold, I Myself will search for My sheep....and will deliver them from all the places to which they were scattered....I will judge between one sheep and another. Then I will set over them one shepherd...he will feed them himself and be their shepherd'" (Ezekiel 34:11-23).

The Lord promised Israel a Son of David, a Shepherd who would feed the sheep Himself. That Shepherd is Jesus. He literally feeds His sheep *Himself.* He feeds them as "The bread of life....the living bread that came down out of heaven" (John 6:48-51). Jesus said, "If anyone eats of this bread, he shall live forever; and the bread also which I shall give for the life of the world is My flesh" (John 6:51). This is the reason the Father judges between one sheep and another, for only those who partake of this "bread of life" receive eternal life.

THE LOST SHEEP OF ISRAEL

The Sheep Hear His Voice

The sheep of Israel know both the voice of their Shepherd and His rest. Jesus said: "My sheep hear My voice, and I know them, and they follow Me; and I give eternal life to them, and they shall never perish" (John 10:27-28). [3] Jesus foretold this coming rest when He said: "I will feed My flock and I will lead them to rest....Then they will know that I, the Lord their God, am with them, and that they, the house of Israel, are My people....[they are] My sheep, the sheep of My pasture" (Ezekiel 34:15,30-31).

One Flock

When in the Garden, Jesus declared: "I have *other sheep*, which are not of this fold; I must bring them also, and they shall hear My voice; and they shall become one flock with one shepherd" (John 10:16).

Jesus said He had sheep who were not of *this fold*, indicating a small enclosed courtyard, a small gathering of sheep. [4] However, He said He would bring His other sheep, and together, they shall be one *flock*, or one large gathering of sheep. [5] In fulfillment of this prophecy, Jesus has, for the past 1900 years, continued to gather the other sheep of Israel.

Caiaphas, the high priest, prophesied "that Jesus was going to die for the nation, and not for the nation only, but that He might also gather together into one the children of God who are scattered abroad" (John 11:51-52).

Before Jesus died on the Cross, He prayed: "I do not ask in behalf of these alone, but for those also who believe in Me through their [the apostles'] word; that they may all be one;

71 ❧

even as Thou, Father, art in Me, and I in Thee, that they also may be in Us" (John 17:20-21).

The Testimony of Unity

Jesus said He desired this unity so "that the world may believe that Thou [Father] didst send Me" (John 17:21). The people of God were to be gathered into one nation—Israel. Our unity as that people was to be the testimony to all the world that God Himself did send Jesus! That means any denial of the unity Jesus prayed for is a denial of both His message and His mission! It is a denial of His very life!

The Lord called forth a single people in the nation of Israel. He made it clear that He would multiply that people through the giving of a Son, a Son who would gather His lost sheep.

However, not all Israelites responded to His call. Therefore, there remain to this day...

17
TWO HOUSES OF ISRAEL

ֲ Both the Church and the Jewish people are Israel, because in the Scriptures there were, and there still are,

Two Houses of Israel!

Both. Two. Two houses of Israel. God speaks "to both the houses of Israel" (Isaiah 8:14). He refers to them as "these two nations" (Ezekiel 35:10). He addresses them as "the two families which the Lord chose" (Jeremiah 33:24).

Two houses. Two nations. Two families chosen for a purpose: "The whole house of Israel and the whole house of Judah...[were] to be my people for my renown and praise and honor. But they have not listened" (Jeremiah 13:11, NIV). Instead, God said both "the house of Israel and the house of

Judah have broken My covenant which I made with their fathers" (Jeremiah 11:10).

Both houses broke His covenant. Both were scattered. In 722 B.C., Ephraim was carried away to Assyria. In 586 B.C., Judah was exiled to Babylon. They were scattered as two separate houses and they *remained* two separate houses!

We see their continued separation confirmed in the Books of Kings, thought to be written between 562 and 538. [1] It says: "So the people of Israel were taken from their homeland into exile in Assyria, and they are *still* there" (2 Kings 17:23, NIV).

They were still separated at approximately 520 B.C. [2] At that time Zechariah spoke of God breaking the "staff called Union, breaking the brotherhood between Judah and Israel" (Zechariah 11:14, NIV). The *NIV Study Bible* says this action is "signifying the dissolution of...the unity between the south and the north." [3] The book *The Twelve Prophets* from *The Soncino Books of the Bible* translates the name of the broken staff, "Binders," and says: "The...staff *Binders*, is now shattered, denoting the dissolution of all unity and harmony between Israel and Judah." [4]

Ezra confirmed these peoples were still separated around 440 B.C. [5] He said the Northern Tribes were scattered in "Halah, Habor, Hara, and to the river Gozan, *to this day* " (1 Chronicles 5:26). Ezra's words were written more than 250 years after the Ephraimites were scattered, and more than fifty years after the people of Judah had returned from Babylon to rebuild the Temple.

Daniel, while still in Babylon with his Jewish people, confirmed the existence of two separate houses. He said, "Righteousness belongs to Thee, O Lord, but to us open shame, as it is this day—to the men of *Judah*, the inhabitants of Jerusalem, and *all Israel*, those who are nearby and those who are far away in all the countries to which Thou hast driven them" (Daniel 9:7). *Judah* was *near*, but according to the *ArtScroll Series*: "All of Israel would mean the ten tribes of Israel who were exiled and lost." [6]

The Lost Tribes?

Were the Ephraimites lost among the nations?

Some say no because Judah, upon their return from Babylon, offered sacrifices on behalf of the twelve tribes. However, *representation* at the sacrifice does not imply all had returned. The people of Judah were well represented at the sacrifices, yet most of them remained behind in Babylon. Even so, those who remained in Babylon continued to be part of Israel—*as did the Ephraimites*—the majority of whom were scattered like seed among the nations.

Some say because the words "all Israel" were used when speaking of those present at the sacrifices, none were lost: "Then Ezra rose and made the leading priests, the Levites, and *all Israel*, take an oath...so *they* took the oath" (Ezra 10:5). The term "all Israel" defines "they." Certainly we would not assert that only *they* who took the oath continued to be the people of Israel.

The term "all Israel" is also used in reference to the Northern Kingdom: "And it came about when *all Israel* heard that Jeroboam had returned, that they sent and called him to the assembly and made him king over *all Israel*. None but the tribe of Judah followed the house of David" (1 Kings 12:20). Here "all Israel" definitely excludes Judah. In both cases the term represents only those who were present.

The argument that the Jewish people who returned were sometimes called "Israel" does not mean the two houses were reunited. While the name "Israel" was primarily used to designate the Ephraimites, it was also used to describe all the sons of Jacob: "The Lord commanded the sons of Jacob, whom He named *Israel* " (2 Kings 17:34). Thus, both houses could be called Israel.

Furthermore, after Judah returned, the Scriptures continued to call them Judah. Ezra 4:4 says the agitators "discouraged the people of Judah" from building. Those who returned were called "the Jewish remnant that survived the exile" (Nehemiah 1:2, NIV). Judah returned from Babylon. Judah rebuilt Jerusalem. The Ephraimites remained lost.

Sinless Israel—United in the King

In the latter days God declares that He *will* unite the two houses: "I will make them one nation in the land...one king will be king for all of them; and they will no longer be two nations, and they will no longer be divided into two kingdoms and they will no longer defile themselves with their idols, or with their detestable things, or with *any* of their transgressions" (Ezekiel 37:22-23).

" 'In those days, at that time,' declares the Lord, 'the people of Israel *and* the people of Judah together will go in tears to seek the Lord their God. They will ask the way to Zion and turn their faces toward it. They will come and bind themselves to the Lord in an everlasting covenant that will not be forgotten....In those days, at that time,' declares the Lord, 'search will be made for Israel's guilt, but there will be none, and for the sins of Judah, but none will be found, for I will forgive the remnant I spare' " (Jeremiah 50:4-5,20, NIV).

Fulfillment of these Scriptures demands that there be *no iniquity—no sin—not in either house!*

Never since the scattering of these two houses have these

Scriptures been fulfilled. From the time of their scattering, the two houses have never been one nation in the land, nor have they ever had a Davidic king over them. [7] Most important, God said *after* He makes them one nation, *the people will no longer defile themselves with their sins and transgressions.*

These Scriptures speak of a *united, sinless Israel*! They speak of a future time when Messiah will reign in Spirit and in truth as the one promised King. But until then, there are still... *Two Houses Of Israel!*

Not All Israelites Are Jews

We must realize that not all of Israel was, or is, called Judah! This point is so important that it bears repeating: Judah does not represent all of Israel!

The two houses of Israel still exist!

18
BOTH HOUSES HAVE STUMBLED

&. Isaiah spoke of the day when the Lord Himself would become a *sanctuary*. He said: "Then He shall become a sanctuary" (Isaiah 8:14). A sanctuary is a holy place, a temple. Jesus said of Himself: "Destroy this temple [sanctuary], and in three days I will raise it up" (John 2:19). Jesus called Himself a *temple*, the *sanctuary* of Isaiah. However, Isaiah warned us: "Then He shall become a sanctuary; *but to both the houses of Israel*, a stone to strike and a rock to stumble over" (Isaiah 8:14). Both houses of Israel stumble over the sanctuary. Both Judah and Ephraim stumble over Jesus!

As a whole, [1] the Jewish people have stumbled over the Suffering Servant, Jesus. They were looking for the Lion of Judah—the Reigning King.

In regard to their brother, Judah, the Church (Ephraim) also has stumbled over the Messiah. They have stumbled through their continued persecution of the Jewish people.

In defense some say, "But those who mistreated the Jews were not *true* Christians. True Christians would not persecute the Jewish people." However, history reveals that many church fathers were true anti-Semites; even as was Martin Luther. [2]

When a person accepts the Lord, he begins a walk of salvation. He is *being* saved. [3] He is being conformed to the image of the Messiah. And many, many Christians have not been perfected in their attitudes toward, and relationships with, the Jewish people. In the name of Jesus, many so-called Christians have harassed the Jewish people, branding them "Christ killers."

However, Jesus said of Himself: "The Son of Man will be betrayed to the chief priests and teachers of the law. They will condemn Him to death and will turn him over to the Gentiles to be mocked and flogged and crucified" (Matthew 20:18-19). Gentiles *also* crucified Jesus. Roman soldiers nailed Jesus to the cross; Roman soldiers abused Him (John 19:23; Luke 23:33-39). Peter and John said, "Indeed Herod and Pontius Pilate met together with the Gentiles and the people of Israel in this city to conspire against your holy servant Jesus" (Acts 4:27, NIV). Jews and Gentiles alike crucified Jesus. And yet Jesus said of Himself: "I lay down My life for the sheep....No one has taken it away from Me, but I lay it down on My own initiative" (John 10:15,18).

Jesus made it clear that He laid down His life because of His love for mankind. Still, for 1900 years the Church has blamed the Jewish people for His death! In this way the Church has *stumbled* over the Messiah.

Our record as the Church is tarnished. It is stained. The Church desires to be the Bride of the Messiah, but there is a Jewish blood stain on her gown. It is a blood stain that must be washed away with true tears of repentance. With truly repentant hearts, Christians must seek the forgiveness of the Jewish people, showing them the fruit of repentance.

Repentant Ephraim

God speaks of Ephraim's day of repentance. He said He "heard Ephraim grieving." Then, Ephraim said, "After I strayed, I repented; after I came to understand, I beat my breast. I was ashamed and humiliated because I bore the disgrace of my youth" (Jeremiah 31:19, NIV).

Part of the youthful reproach of the people of Ephraim (the Church) is that they fostered hatred toward the Jewish people. However, in time, Ephraim will repent of his transgression against Judah. Ephraim will recall that Jesus was Himself a Jew, that He wept over Jerusalem and that He loves His Jewish people—*as Jews* (John 4:22; Luke 19:41).

Jesus loves the Jews.

Jesus also loves the Ephraimites.

Furthermore, Jesus longs for the day when the two houses will be reconciled in Him. For only God's ideal—a sinless, undivided House of Israel—will enter into eternity in the presence of God.

Nonetheless, a bitter contention has long existed between the two houses. But why?

19
YANKEES AND REBELS

&. Years before entering into the Promised Land, twelve men, one representing each of the twelve tribes, were sent to spy out the Land. Only two, Joshua and Caleb, returned with a good report. Later, these two led the people into the Promised Land.

According to Numbers 13, Caleb was from the tribe of Judah, and Joshua was from the tribe of Ephraim. Allegorically, there were two witnesses giving a good report regarding the promises of God: a Judahite and an Ephraimite.

The Book of Revelation also speaks of two witnesses: It says, "I will grant the power of prophecy to My two witnesses" (Revelation 11:3, TAB). Here we see the two witnesses are anointed to speak for God. Also, God describes them as: "The two olive trees...that stand before the Lord of the whole earth" (Revelation 11:4). When Zechariah asked God: "What are these two olive trees"? (Zechariah 4:11, NIV), God answered: "These are the two who are anointed to serve the Lord of all the earth" (Zechariah 4:14, NIV). Metaphorically, we see the two witnesses are two anointed olive trees that speak for God.

In Romans 11, another reference is made to two olive branches. Those gathered from the nations are represented by a "wild olive branch" and those from Judah by a "natural olive branch." Two branches. Two witnesses. Two houses.

Returning to the two houses, we see Israel was united under three successive kings. First there was Saul, a Benjaminite. Following him, God raised up the house of David. David was king over all Israel, for "all Israel *and* Judah loved David" (1 Samuel 18:16).

Solomon followed his father David as king. But Solomon entered into sin by building places of idol worship for his foreign wives. His idolatry sounded the death knell for the unified Kingdom of Israel. The Lord said: "Because you have done this...I will surely tear the kingdom from you, and will give it to your servant. Nevertheless I will not do it in your days for the sake of your father David, but I will tear it out of the hand of your son" (1 Kings 11:11-12).

Judah, the Beloved

The kingdom was torn from Solomon's son because of idolatry. "However, [God said] I will not tear away *all* the kingdom, but I will give one tribe to your son for the sake of My servant David and for the sake of Jerusalem which I have chosen" (1 Kings 11:13).

Following the partitioning, Judah remained a kingdom because they were beloved for the sake of their father, David, and because of God's love for Jerusalem, His chosen city. That status remains unchanged. Romans 11:28 says of the Jew: "From the standpoint of God's choice, they are beloved for the sake of the fathers."

Divided Ten to One

Nonetheless, the greater portion of the kingdom was taken from Judah's sovereignty when God declared to Jeroboam: "I am going to tear the kingdom out of Solomon's hand and give you ten tribes" (1 Kings 11:26, NIV).

Ten parts of the kingdom were given to Jeroboam. [1] Thus, the kingdom of Israel was torn in two—divided by the Almighty. God Himself said of the division: "This thing has come from Me" (1 Kings 12:24).

The Israelites actually separated into two houses after King Solomon's rule. The division can be compared to that of the United States during the Civil War—Yankees and Rebels —North and South. While all remained Americans, the battle raged, brother fighting against brother. The same was true with Israel. The southern kingdom, Judah, and the northern kingdom, Ephraim, repeatedly warred against each other.

Ironically, one reason for their separation was a type of slave labor. Many in the house of Joseph had become conscripted laborers for the ruling house of Judah. [2]

King Solomon needed an overseer to control these forced laborers. When he recognized "the man Jeroboam was a valiant warrior, and when Solomon saw that the young man was industrious, he appointed him over all the forced labor of the house of Joseph" (1 Kings 11:28). However, after the Lord revealed to Solomon that Jeroboam would receive ten tribes, Solomon sought to kill him. Fleeing to Egypt, Jeroboam remained there until Solomon's death.

After Solomon's death, his son, "Rehoboam went to Shechem, for all the Israelites had gone there to make him king. When Jeroboam son of Nebat heard this (he was still in Egypt, where he had fled from King Solomon), he returned from Egypt. So they sent for Jeroboam, and he and the whole assembly of Israel went to Rehoboam and said to him: 'Your father put a heavy yoke on us, but now lighten the harsh labor and the heavy yoke he put on us and we will serve you' " (1 Kings 12:1-4, NIV). Rehoboam ignored the wise counsel of the elders to relent. Instead, he listened to his peers to make the service even harsher. God said of the king's refusal to listen: "It was a turn of events from the Lord, that He might establish His word...to Jeroboam the son of Nebat" (1 Kings 12:15).

The reappearance of Jeroboam prompted Rehoboam to make his move to retake all Israel. Then "King Rehoboam sent Adoram, who was over the forced labor, [apparently he had taken Jeroboam's place] and all Israel [the Ephraimites] stoned him to death. And King Rehoboam made haste to mount his chariot to flee to [his capital] Jerusalem" (1 Kings 12:18).

"It came about when all Israel [the Northern Kingdom] heard that Jeroboam had returned, that they sent and called him to the assembly and made him king over all Israel [the Northern Kingdom]" (1 Kings 12:20).

The Kingdom of Israel was thus divided. Rehoboam was King of Judah, and Jeroboam was King of Ephraim. While on the surface the cause appeared to be forced labor, there was a much deeper problem. It is a problem that continues to plague Ephraim and Judah even today. It is a contention that began in Genesis.

20
THE DIVIDED BLESSING

&. The contention between Ephraim and Judah stems from a misunderstanding of Jacob's blessing.

We have seen that God gave Jacob His two-fold plan of fruitfulness for Israel, which was the single nation, and the congregation of nations. This blessing was divided between Manasseh and Ephraim—Old and New Covenant Israel.

In addition, Jacob received from Isaac the title of first-born. As such, he became the preeminent one. [1] However, when Jacob conveyed his blessing, he divided it between two peoples.

Four thousand years ago, Jacob divided his first-born blessing between two peoples, and it has been the cause of war ever since.

How was it divided? Why did it cause a war?

Thus far, we have seen Joseph's *double portion* blessing

fulfilled through "Ephraim the First-born." But we have not yet accounted for the blessing of...

Preeminence

After Jacob blessed Joseph, he called his other sons together and said: "Assemble yourselves that I may tell you what shall befall you in the days to come....Reuben, you are my first-born; my might and the beginning of my strength, preeminent in dignity and preeminent in power. Uncontrolled as water, you shall not have *preeminence*." Turning to Simeon and Levi, he said: "Let not my glory be united with their assembly; because in their anger they slew men" (Genesis 49:1-6).

The first three sons failed to receive preeminence because of sin. Jacob then said to his fourth son: "Judah, your brothers shall praise you; your hand shall be on the neck of your enemies; your father's sons shall bow down to you. Judah is a lion's whelp; from the prey, my son, you have gone up. He couches, he lies down as a lion, and as a lion, who dares rouse him up? The scepter shall not depart from Judah, nor the ruler's staff from between his feet, until Shiloh comes, and to him shall be the obedience of the peoples" (Genesis 49:8-10).

As stated earlier, the first-born was due respect as leader among the brothers. To him belonged preeminence and sovereignty. He was the family ruler. And Jacob said of Judah: "Your brothers shall bow down to you." Jacob called Judah a kingly lion, the symbol of royalty. He said the scepter, symbol of royal authority, shall not depart from Judah.

Among the sons of Israel, Judah was established as the sovereign—and sovereignty was one of the two gifts that belonged to the first-born.

Sibling Rivalry

Jacob gave Joseph the double portion and he gave Judah preeminence. A war began over this division. It is a war that began in the deserts of the Sinai, a war of sibling rivalry that continues even today.

This rivalry, this war, continues because both houses covet a title for themselves! Both covet the glory and position it brings for themselves.

Because of rivalry, the people of Judah refuse to recognize the Ephraimites as legitimate, equal heirs of Israel. [2] In turn, the Ephraimites respond in violence and anger, seeking to deny and destroy the people of Judah. [3] Each of these battling brothers, in their own way, seeks to eliminate the other. Each wants the title for themselves—that *they* might be exalted.

But with God, the title of First-born Israel belongs to One who does not exalt Himself. It belongs both to "Ephraim the First-born" and to "His seed." And only when we seek to be conformed to His image can any of us share in His double portion.

On the other hand, if "Ephraim the First-born" is so clearly Jacob's heir, why was Joseph given the double portion and Judah given preeminence?

O Jacob, Jacob, did you have a special hidden meaning in the division of your blessing? Why did you declare Ephraim to be the First-born and yet give preeminence to Judah? O Jacob, Jacob, did you know your blessing would start a war?

21
JACOB KNEW

❧ Jacob understood the inheritance due the first-born. He knew better than anyone else how hard people would fight for the title. It was he who deliberately deceived his father into giving the blessing to him rather than Esau. Both Jacob and his mother, Rebekah, knew the importance of the blessing.

However, if Jacob, when conveying this blessing, meant Ephraim, the son of Joseph, then we must question his actions. We must question him, because after giving Ephraim the double portion, Jacob gave the family sovereignty to Judah!

Surely Jacob must have realized these two would war over this divided blessing. With Ephraim having the title of first-born, small wonder he was constantly warring with the older Judah, who had the family sovereignty.

Did Jacob intend to start a war between siblings? Did he want his descendants to fight over his blessing? Or did Jacob see something far greater than earthly first-born blessing? Did he have a higher motive than ever has been attributed to him? Could this be the reason God so honored Jacob as to call Himself "The God of Jacob"? Did God look into his heart and see that, although misguided in the way he chose to obtain the blessing, by faith he understood the significance of being Isaac's first-born?

Surely Jacob knew of God's promise: That through the seed of his father would come The Seed, the Messiah of Israel! And through Him would finally come the great congregation of peoples promised to his fathers.

We know Jacob met the God-Man: The True First-born. Jacob said: "I have seen God face to face" (Genesis 32:30). After encountering the True Israel, Jacob began to be conformed to His image. Thus Jacob became Israel.

Jacob met the only One who is truly capable of being God's Powerful, Prevailing Prince. Having met Him, Jacob understood his blessing was so enormous that only One could ever truly fulfill its high calling.

Jacob understood that others must also meet and wrestle with the First-born Man. He knew that only through prevailing in Him, through being conformed to His image, would his descendants become the earth-shaking congregation promised to his fathers. Only then could they truly be Israel.

By Faith, Jacob Blessed

Jacob is listed in the famous "hall of faith" found in the eleventh chapter of Hebrews. It says of him: "By faith Jacob, as he was dying, blessed each of *the sons of Joseph,* and worshipped, leaning on the top of his staff " (Hebrews 11:21).

Jacob was a great man of faith because he blessed *the sons of*

Joseph—Manasseh and Ephraim—Old and New Covenant Israel!

By faith, Jacob knew the blessing of Israel had a higher and greater call than just the literal, single Old Covenant tribe of Manasseh. He knew it was greater than just the Ten Tribes of Ephraim. By faith, Jacob knew his blessing was to be carried to *all* nations. He knew his blessing encompassed both covenants of Israel.

How can this be asserted with such confidence?

The Apostle Peter declares: "The prophets who prophesied of the grace that would come to you made careful search and inquiry, seeking to know what person or time the Spirit of Christ within them was indicating....It was revealed to them that they were not serving themselves, but you, in these things which now have been announced to you through those who preached the gospel by the Holy Spirit sent from heaven" (1 Peter 1:10-12).

Jacob prophesied of the great blessings that would come to Manasseh and Ephraim, and the prophets sought to know the person and the time the Spirit was indicating.

Also, speaking of the great men of faith (including Jacob), Hebrews says: "And *all* these, having gained approval through their faith, *did not receive what was promised*, because God had provided something better for us, so that apart from *us* they should not be made perfect" (Hebrews 11:39-40). Apart from us, Jacob did not receive what was promised, nor was his blessing of Manasseh and Ephraim truly fulfilled. Without *us*, the blessing is not complete.

Yes, Jacob knew there was something better. He had met the First-born One face to face. He knew the One through Whom all the nations would be blessed.

Jacob knew. But many of his sons do not know.

Two brothers continue to war over the blessing of the first-born, each coveting the preeminent position for himself.

22
THE MYSTERY OF THE FIRST-BORN

  🙋 Jacob told his sons: "The blessings of thy father...shall be on the head of Joseph" (Genesis 49:26, KJV). This blessing was next given to Ephraim, and yet Judah prevailed. How can Ephraim have Israel's first-born blessing, if Judah has the preeminence?

  This mystery is unveiled when we see that Judah's blessing was *conditional.* Jacob said Judah would be preeminent *"until* Shiloh comes, and to him shall be the obedience of the peoples" (Genesis 49:10).

  Shiloh is the High Priest, the Prince, the Lion of Judah. [1] He is Jesus, the Man with many names.

  Through this blessing, Jacob blessed Judah with a role in bringing forth the True First-born. The tribe of Judah is truly privileged to have such a One descend from them. The Holy One of Israel came to this earth as a man. He came as a Jew.

In accordance with the Law of Moses, Jesus was presented in the Temple as a first-born son from the tribe of Judah (Luke 2:21-24). Because of this, the tribe of Judah was honored above all the peoples on the face of the earth. This privilege by itself makes Judah forever preeminent among the nations. No other tribe of peoples will ever be so honored as is Judah.

However, "though Judah was the strongest of his brothers and a ruler came from him, the rights of the firstborn belonged to Joseph" (1 Chronicles 5:2, NIV).

How can this be explained?

Jacob did not give his first-born inheritance to Judah, to the physical Ephraim, nor to any of their descendants. But he made the benefits of the first-born blessing available to all of them.

How this was accomplished becomes clear through a study of two of Jesus' titles: The *Only* Begotten Son, and, The First-born of *Many*.

The Only Begotten Son

Jesus came to this earth as a particular type of man. He came as "the only begotten from the Father" (John 1:14). To us, "God...gave His only begotten Son" (John 3:16).

In Greek, the word for only begotten is *monogenes*, meaning sole, single, unique, only-born. [2] Jesus is the unique, only begotten Son of God. However, He was not *begotten* in the sense of being *created*. When God said of Jesus, "Thou art My Son, today I have *begotten* Thee" (Psalms 2:7); the word being used is *yalad*. It is used in the sense of the father helping a baby to be born. [3] It is not used in the sense of created, because Jesus is the One "who is and who was and who is to come, the Almighty" (Revelation 1:8). He is the great "I AM"

(John 8:58). Father God uses the term *yalad* because He helped bring Jesus forth as a human child—and in this role, Jesus is His only begotten Son.

As the only begotten Son, Jesus came as the fulfillment of the promise given to Judah. He came as Shiloh, taking the preeminence from Judah.

Then, the King of the Jews offered Himself as a Sacrifice. As prophesied in Psalm 22, the only Begotten Son of God died on the Tree.

But this Lion from the tribe of Judah has overcome (Revelation 5:5). Through His sacrifice, He overcame sin, and then...He rose again! However, Jesus rose again as a different type of man.

The First-born of Many Brethren

When Jesus was resurrected, He arose from the grave as Ephraim The First-born—the son of the double portion—the first man to have life in this world and life in the world to come. And, He arose as the First-born of *many* brethren.

As stated earlier, in the case of the patriarchs, it took an act of divine intervention to bring forth the first-born. While the Scriptures record no such action in the birth of the physical Ephraim, there was divine intervention in bringing forth God's First-born Ephraim. When Jesus was conceived as a man-child, God Himself opened His mother Mary's womb. After He was offered as a sacrifice, again it was through a great act of divine intervention that He was brought forth. This time however, God opened the womb of the grave! This was in fulfillment of God's promise to the people of Ephraim: "I will ransom them from the power of the grave; I will redeem them from death. Where, O death, are your plagues? Where, O grave, is your destruction?" (Hosea 13:14, NIV). The plague of

97 ❧

death was removed when Jesus was resurrected, for He was resurrected as The First Immortal Man!

This resurrection of the First-born was foretold by David, through whom God declared: "I also shall make Him My first-born" (Psalm 89:27). *Make* in the Hebrew is *natan*, meaning to give, to make, to lift up, to bring forth; to ordain, to appoint. [4] God chose this word because the Spirit of God lifted Jesus up on the third day. God brought Him forth from the grave, appointing Him as the First-born—the One ordained to be given the nations.

In this role Jesus is Ephraim, the First-born of many brethren. For since Jesus opened the gates of glory, many have followed Him as eternal brethren; many have shared in His double portion.

Through these two separate roles Jesus was the fulfillment of the promises to both Judah and Ephraim. The *only* begotten Son was the fulfillment of the blessing to Judah. The first-born of *many* brethren is the fulfillment of the blessing given to Ephraim.

United in Messiah Jesus

Jacob's divided blessing was reunited in Messiah Jesus. Paul said of Him: "He Himself is our peace, who made both groups into one " (Ephesians 2:14). God planned that through Jesus, "He might make the two into one new man, thus establishing peace" (Ephesians 2:15).

In Jesus, the barrier of the dividing wall, the enmity, between Ephraim and Judah—Jew and Gentile—has been abolished (Ephesians 2:14).

It is God's desire that there be peace in the New Covenant House of Israel; therefore He did not exalt one people over another. Although each physical heir was allowed to play a special role—the true heir is Jesus.

Jacob did not give his precious blessing to mortal men only. Jacob knew no mere mortal man could in himself fulfill the high calling of Israel. He knew it could only be fulfilled when a person encounters and is truly transformed into the image of the First-born.

When your soul and character become like that of Jesus, then you are Israel.

23
THE BLOOD

❧ In the Scriptures there are two people called *Israel*: Jacob and Jesus. These two Israels have two different "blood types": the human blood of Jacob, and the divine blood of Jesus. The difference in these two blood types becomes apparent through a study of the *seed*.

The promises spoken to Abraham "were spoken...to one ...that is, Christ" (Galatians 3:16). Before fulfilling this promise, God wanted His people to see their sin. Therefore, the Law was given to point out our transgressions, "until the seed should come to whom the promise had been made" (Galatians 3:19).

Jesus is the Seed *to whom* the promise was made. The Law was given that it might "become our tutor to lead us to Christ, that we may be justified by faith" (Galatians 3:24). The purpose of the Law was, and is, to reveal our sin. In fact, the Scriptures that gave the Law, "shut up all men under sin, that *the promise...might be given to those who believe*" (Galatians 3:22). The promise spoken of is the Seed.

The Seed of Faith

Because Abraham believed God, he was given the promise of the Seed. Likewise, when we have the same faith, we receive the promised Seed: We become "sons of God through faith in Christ Jesus" (Galatians 3:26). Through faith, we are born from above—becoming heirs of Abraham's promise: "If you belong to Christ, then you are Abraham's offspring, heirs according to promise" (Galatians 3:29).

As the seed of Adam, we must be born from above because death reigns in our human blood. Regardless of our ancestry, we are doomed to death.

God, in His mercy, planned to redeem man from this curse through faith in the blood of Jesus. Through faith in His sacrifice, the sins of man could be removed, remitted, literally taken away.

The blood of Adam (mankind) could not remove sin, because it is death-filled. [1] The blood of animal sacrifices only *covered*, or *atoned* for sins. [2] But the sinless blood of Jesus provided *remittance* for sin: a complete *removal* of the cause of offense. [3] The blood of Jesus can remove sin because it is sinless blood.

The Death-Filled Blood of Adam

Genesis tells us, "The Lord God formed the man from the dust of the ground." *Then*, He "breathed into his nostrils the breath of life, and the man became a living being" (Genesis 2:7, NIV). God made Adam's body from the ground, but he was not a living being until God breathed into him *the breath of life*. The breath of life God breathed into him must have been blood, because it was life, and the Word says, "life is in the blood" (Leviticus 17:11).

When Adam sinned, corruption entered into his life-blood. God warned Adam not to eat of the tree: "For in the day that you eat from it you shall surely die" (Genesis 2:17). Adam ate from the tree, and the sin caused a type of "blood poisoning." [4] Since we all descend from Adam, we *all* suffer from this blood poisoning. Because God "made from one [blood], every nation of mankind to live on all the...earth" (Acts 17:26).

Every one of us, without exception, is destined to die. Everyone: Jew, Gentile, bond, or free, we all are corrupted by the blood of Adam.

Everyone except Jesus.

The Sinless Blood of Jesus

Jesus is the exception because He was not born of the blood of Adam. He was the "Son of Adam," the "Son of Man," the "Son of Mary," and "the Son of David after the flesh," and yet He did not partake of Adam's death-filled blood (Luke 3:38; Matthew 19:28; Mark 6:3; 12:35; Romans 1:3).

God sent His "Son in the likeness of sinful flesh"; still, Jesus "knew no sin" (Romans 8:3; 2 Corinthians 5:21). How could Jesus come in the likeness of "sinful flesh" and remain "without sin"? How could He be the Son of Adam but not have the blood of Adam? Herein lies another mystery.

Jesus said to the Father: "You have made ready a body for

Me [to offer]" (Hebrews 10:5, TAB). The word translated *made ready*, means to *adjust*, to *prepare*. [5] A body was adjusted for Jesus, that it might be offered to God. How this body was modified to be offered is understood through an understanding of the origin of the blood. In addition, the origin of the blood explains the reason for...

The Virgin Birth

Speaking of the earthly conception of the Son of God, Matthew said, "When His mother Mary had been betrothed to Joseph, before they came together she was found to be with child by the Holy Spirit" (Matthew 1:18).

The God of the universe, the One who created the first man from the dust of the earth, allowed His only Son to descend to the earth to be born of a woman. "Now all this took place that what was spoken by the Lord through the prophet might be fulfilled, saying, 'Behold, the virgin shall be with child, and shall bear a Son, and they shall call His Name Immanuel,' which translated means, 'God with us' " (Matthew 1:22-23). [6]

The Son of God was born of a virgin as a sign to God's people that this Child was different. He was different because although He received His *body* from a sinful race, sinful *blood* was not in His body.

The Amplified Bible says, "Great and important and weighty, we confess, is the hidden truth—the mystic secret —of godliness. He (God) was made visible in human flesh" (1 Timothy 3:16). The mystery is that Jesus was a *God-man*. He only "partook," or "took *part* " of humanity (Hebrews 2:14). Jesus had the sinful flesh of man, which was provided by his mother, but He had the sinless blood of His Father.

This was possible because when God created woman, He made her so that one day she could be used to bring forth His sinless Son. God deliberately created woman so that *no blood would pass from mother to child!*

The Origin of the Blood

In his book, *The Chemistry of the Blood, M.R. DeHann, M.D.*, explains the origin of the blood:

> The blood which flows in an unborn babe's arteries and veins is not derived from the mother but is produced within the body of the foetus....It is only after the sperm has entered the ovum and a foetus begins to develop that blood appears.
>
> As a very simple illustration of this, think of the egg of a hen. An unfertilized egg is simply an ovum on a much larger scale than the human ovum. You may incubate this unfertilized hen's egg, but it will never develop. It will dry up completely but no chick will result. But let that egg be fertilized by the introduction of the male sperm and incubation will bring to light the presence of life in an embryo. After a few hours it visibly develops. In a little while red streaks occur, denoting the presence of blood...
>
> According to scientists...from the time of conception to the time of birth...not ONE SINGLE DROP OF BLOOD ever passes from mother to child.... *The mother contributes no blood at all.* [7]

The blood is not conveyed by the mother; rather, it is conveyed by the seed of the father!

The textbooks confirm DeHaan's findings. *The New Encyclopaedia Britannica* says, "Centrioles...[are] apparently supplied by the sperm." [8] *Webster's Dictionary* defines a centriole as, "the center of a centrosome" [9] and a centrosome as "a minute protoplasmic body." [10] *Plasma* is "the fluid part of blood",[11] and *protoplasma* is "organized living matter: the...fluid...complex of...the living nucleus...that is...*often designated the physical basis of life."* ! [12]

The basis of life is in the father's protoplasmic seed: a seed made of fluid and plasma—water and blood.

Jesus came by just such a seed. John tells us there is "one who came *by water and blood*—Jesus Christ" (1 John 5:6, NIV).

Long ago, God prepared for His Son to be born of a virgin, of a Seed from above. Thus could God create a second Adam, a Son of Adam after the flesh, with the sinless blood of His Heavenly Father flowing in His veins. [13] Thus did God adjust a body for His Son—a body that was worthy as a sin offering.

The Eternal Blood Sacrifice

"The life of the flesh is in the blood, and I have given it to you on the altar to make atonement for your souls, for it is the blood by reason of the life that makes atonement" (Leviticus 17:11). For "without shedding of blood there is no forgiveness" (Hebrews 9:22).

As our High Priest, Messiah Jesus entered the heavenly Holy of Holies and sprinkled it with His blood (Hebrews 9:23-26). Because His blood is sinless, it did more than just cover our sins—it literally did away with them. By His sacrifice in our behalf, we are justified, made righteous—therefore we can live eternally in the presence of God. For "by one offering He has perfected for all time those who are sanctified" (Hebrews 10:14).

When we ask Him to be our High Priest, we are "justified by His blood" (Romans 5:9). Our spirit-man is then born anew of

God's "imperishable seed" (1 Peter 1:23). In this way we are given a new blood type! The blood of our heavenly Father flows through our spiritual veins! Like Him, we are eternal beings —our names are written in the Book of Life.

And thus we become...

24
THE ISRAEL OF GOD

&. The Kingdom of Israel and the Kingdom of God are one and the same. This is evident in that God said to David regarding his Seed: "I will establish the throne of *his* kingdom forever...[And thus] your throne [David] shall be established forever" (2 Samuel 7:13,16). Speaking of this same Son, the angel Gabriel told Mary: "The Lord God will give Him the throne of His father David; and He will reign over the house of Jacob forever; and His Kingdom will have no end" (Luke 1:32-33).

David was king over Jacob's descendants—the Kingdom of Israel. Because the Lord "has given the kingship of Israel to David and his *seed* forever" (2 Chronicles 13:5, NIV). [1] This kingdom is also called "the kingdom of the Lord over Israel" (1 Chronicles 28:5, NIV) and "the Kingdom of Christ and of God" (Ephesians 5:5, NIV).

David's throne and kingship over Israel were given to Jesus: For He "*has taken* His seat at the right hand of the throne of the Majesty" (Hebrews 8:1). We know He currently rules over Israel because He "sat down" (Hebrews 1:3). (One sits on the throne only after taking the Kingdom.)

Further, Jesus "was faithful as a Son over His house" (Hebrews 3:6), and, Luke said, "He will reign over *the house of Jacob.*" Since Jacob is Israel, Jesus' house is the *house of Israel.*

Who constitutes the house of Israel over which Jesus rules? "Christ was faithful as a Son over His house *whose house we are,* if we hold fast our confidence and the boast of our hope firm until the end" (Hebrews 3:6).

This confidence is the courage to enter into the Holy Place. "We have confidence to enter the holy place by the blood of Jesus" (Hebrews 10:19). We can enter the holy place because we are "being built up as a spiritual house for a holy priesthood, to offer up spiritual sacrifices acceptable to God through Jesus Christ" (1 Peter 2:5). As such, we are "a chosen race, a royal priesthood, a holy nation, a people for God's own possession" (1 Peter 2:9).

Natural, New Covenant Israel

As the Israel of God, once again, we must ask: Are we literal, physical Israelites?

As stated previously, under Old Covenant and New, proselytes physically become one with the people of Israel by circumcision, observance of Passover and sojourning. *Based on this criteria, we are indeed natural Israel.*

Secondly, as was established, the bloodline is conveyed by the father. (The male transference of blood line explains the male covenant of circumcision, and the reason Biblical genealogies primarily list only the father.) [2] In addition, the life that was in the Twelve Princes of Israel was in their blood. Today that bloodline is in that of their seed. Exactly where the bloodlines of the tribes of Israel have gone—only God knows.

However, if the Creator of the universe chose to follow that line, it would be a simple thing for Him to do so. Assuming a new generation is produced every forty years, it would take only 100 fathers per person to go back 4,000 years to the time of Abraham.

Remembering 100 fathers per person would be effortless for the God who numbers the hairs of our head.

Surely there are countless millions in the Church who are bloodline descendants of the Twelve Tribes. Surely there are those who are descended from the Apostles. The thousands and thousands of early Church believers must have resulted in millions and millions of descendants.

God told Abraham: "I will *multiply* you *exceedingly*...I will make you the father of a multitude of nations...I will greatly multiply your seed as the stars of the heavens" (Genesis 17:2,5; 22:17). God told Isaac: "I will multiply your descendants as the stars of the heavens" (Genesis 26:4). Rebekah was to be a mother of "thousands of millions" (Genesis 24:60, KJV). God told Jacob: "Be fruitful and multiply" (Genesis 35:11)

Repeatedly, God spoke a blessing of *increase* over the *physical seed* of Abraham, Isaac, and Jacob. By the same token, God said one time, of Abraham's other son: "As for Ishmael, I...will multiply him exceedingly" (Genesis 17:20). Ishmael is the father of the Arab people, who today number approximately 650 million people! [3]

In light of that, how can we possibly believe that the fifteen million Jewish people of today fully represent the *repeatedly* blessed *physical* seed of Abraham, Isaac and Jacob! If today there are only fifteen million identifiable physical descendants of Isaac—and 650 million descendants of Ishmael—then Isaac got only 1.76 per cent of the physical blessing given Ishmael!

The Church must realize it cannot be entirely made up of former Gentiles. Literal millions must be physical descendants of Abraham, Isaac and Jacob! Thus, within the Church there are countless millions of bloodline descendants of Israel!

Eternal Israel

Our third point is the most important: We become one with the *eternal* Israel when we are born of the Seed from above.

The physical seed that comes from Jacob and the Twelve Tribes is doomed to die a mortal death. However, the Seed that comes from above is destined to live forever—*and absolutely no one is related to that Seed by the blood of Adam*! One can become related to that Seed *only* through the "spirit of adoption."

While it is possible for one to be related to the *flesh* that housed the Messiah, such a physical relationship will not save one from spiritual death. To live eternally in the presence of God, one must be born a second time of the Seed from above, becoming the Israel destined to live eternally.

25
THE IRREVOCABLE CALL

    🙪 *The Amplified Bible* says of God's gifts: "He never withdraws them once they are given, and He does not change His mind about those to whom He sends His call" (Romans 11:29).

The descendants of Israel received an irrevocable call to be the people of Israel. However, this calling was both "a blessing and a curse" (Deuteronomy 11:26). In Israel, it is possible to be cursed in your going out and in your coming in, cursed until you perish—or, blessed in your going out and in your coming in, blessed until your blessings overtake you! (Deuteronomy 28:6,19.)

While Israelites are called to reign with God, it is also possible for them to become "the *degenerate* shoots of a foreign vine" (Jeremiah 2:21). However, ultimately God will burn up all degenerate branches (Matthew 7:19).

Until that time, those who deem themselves to be righteous branches should realize that with God...

Knowledge Brings Responsibility

The Scriptures reveal Judah as the more righteous of the two houses. This fact seems only to have angered God all the more with Judah. It was as though Luke 12:48 applied to them: "To whom much is given, of him shall much be required" (TAB).

Judah saw God's judgment fall on "faithless Israel" (Ephraim), yet did not repent. Instead, they foolishly followed in Ephraim's footsteps. Because of this, God says: "Faithless Israel is more righteous than unfaithful Judah" (Jeremiah 3:11, NIV).

This Scripture sounds a solemn warning to the Church of the First-born. Through it God has forever established a principle: *Greater knowledge brings greater responsibility* !

Those who know God are responsible for carrying out His will in the earth. And God clearly revealed His will regarding treatment of Judah during their time of distress. He said: "You should not look down on your brother in the day of his misfortune, nor rejoice over the people of Judah in the day of their destruction, nor boast so much in the day of their trouble" (Obadiah 1:12, NIV). Paul also warned the Church: "Do not be arrogant toward the branches [Judah]." Because you only "stand by your faith. Do not be conceited, but fear; for if God did not spare the natural branches [Judah], neither will He spare you" (Romans 11:18-21). The Almighty has sworn: "Those who harass Judah will be cut off" (Isaiah 11:13).

Beloved Judah—Used by God

Paul said his Jewish people had "stumbled." However, James says, "We *all* stumble in many ways" (James 3:2). Paul asked regarding Judah: "Did they stumble so as to fall beyond *recovery?*" (Romans 11:11, NIV). No; rather, they *tripped*, meaning they lost their spiritual balance. But, they did not fall so as to fall down and not rise again. [1] Judah will rise again; for God says He has *not* rejected them. They will regain their balance—because they are beloved.

Why is Judah the beloved of God? Can it be that God feels compassion for them because He *used* them? Certainly, Judah was used to bring salvation to the Gentiles. Jesus Himself said: "Salvation is from the Jews" (John 4:22). Paul explained that "by their [Judah's] transgression salvation has come to the Gentiles" (Romans 11:11). That means the vehicle for the salvation of the Gentiles was the transgression of the Jew.

In addition, God loves variety; therefore, He created many different peoples. But in order for God to become a man, He *had* to choose one of His many peoples—and He chose to use Judah.

God also used the Jewish people to help Him establish the Law that points His people to the Messiah. Had God wanted to use the Ephraimites for that purpose, He would not have found them willing vessels: "The men of Ephraim...did not keep God's covenant and refused to live by his law" (Psalm 78:9-10, NIV). However, Judah was willing. In fact, Judah has always been the family of Israel that has tried to keep the Law, [2] and therefore, God chose Judah. But they were chosen to be *used*, not to be *exalted*.

Had the Jewish people, as a whole, accepted and established their Jewish Messiah as King of the world, our situation would have been quite different. Jewish people would most definitely have felt exalted.

Realizing this, did God allow the heart of the Jew to be hardened—so that they would not be exalted over their fellow men? Did God allow their necks to become stiff, so that others might be used to install the Jewish Messiah as King of the world?

Yes, God definitely used Judah. Therefore Judah is beloved.

Disobedient Ephraim

In turn, God desires to use the Gentiles. Salvation came to the Gentiles —that they might provoke the Jews—that they might "make them jealous" (Romans 11:11). Once again, we see God seeking an "example" people. This time however, the Ephraimites are to provoke Judah. Speaking to Jewish Israelites, Paul said God would provoke them "to jealousy by them that are not a people." Furthermore God said, "By a foolish nation will I anger you" (Romans 10:19, KJV). In other words, I will make you jealous, Judah, by those who are *foolish Ephraimites*—by those who are *Lo-ammi—not My people.*

The Apostle Paul also told the Church: "Just as you who were at one time disobedient to God have now received mercy as a result of their disobedience...so they too may now receive mercy as a result of God's mercy to you. For God has bound all men over to disobedience so that he may have mercy on them all" (Romans 11:30-32, NIV).

These Scriptures speak of Ephraimites who were at one time disobedient to the Law because, for pagan Gentiles, there was no Law (Romans 4:15). [3] The Scriptures are telling us each house has in turn been disobedient. It is saying that just as the

Ephraimites have obtained mercy through Judah's disobedience, so, too, Judah must now be shown mercy by once-disobedient Ephraim. God clearly states He has shut up all in disobedience; *that He might show mercy to all.*

All have sinned. Both houses. Judah and Ephraim both have been disobedient. But God wants to show mercy to both houses, and He wants both houses to show mercy to one another.

Part of Israel Was Hardened

The Amplified Bible reveals God's plan of merciful salvation for both houses: "Lest you be self-opinionated—wise in your own conceits—I do not want you to miss this hidden truth and mystery, brethren: a hardening (insensibility) has [temporarily] befallen *a part of Israel* [to last] until the full number of the ingathering of the Gentiles has come in, and so all Israel will be saved" (Romans 11:25-26).

The mystery is: a hardening has befallen *a part of Israel.* Judah was hardened until Ephraim could be gathered! Thus, we see God's plan to save all Israel!

One day Judah will no longer be hardened: "Now if their [Judah's] transgression be riches for the world and their failure be riches for the Gentiles [those of Ephraim], how much more will their fulfillment be!" (Romans 11:12).

More, much more! It will be a glorious day of splendor and blessing for both houses. When Judah is no longer blinded to the Messiah, and Ephraim is no longer blinded to their identity, it will be glorious!

However, until that day, those who know the Messiah of Israel must remember God's principle: *Greater knowledge brings greater responsibility* ! We who know more are responsible for bringing about the reconciliation our Father desires among His people Israel.

26
THE LATTER DAYS

    ❧ Just as King David ruled over *all* Israel, so one day Jesus also will be King over all Israel: " 'At that time,' declares the Lord, 'I will be the God of *all* the families of Israel, and they shall be My people' " (Jeremiah 31:1).

God has a latter-day plan to unite the two houses: "Thus says the Lord of hosts, 'In those days ten men from all the nations will grasp the garment of a Jew saying, 'Let us go with you, for we have heard that God is with you' " (Zechariah 8:23).

Ten men will grab hold of *one* Jew. These numbers were used when God said to Jeroboam, "I...give you *ten* tribes...but to his son [David's] I will give *one* tribe" (1 Kings 11:31,36). Ten to one. Ephraim outnumbered Judah ten to one: "The sons of Israel were 300,000, and the men of Judah 30,000" (1 Samuel 11:8).

"In those days the house of *Judah* will walk with the house of *Israel*, and *they* will come together from the land of the north to the land that I gave your fathers as an inheritance" (Jeremiah 3:18).

"It will come about in that day that the nations will resort to the root of Jesse....then it will happen on that day that the Lord will again recover the *second* time with His hand the remnant of His people....And He will lift up a standard for the nations, and will assemble the banished ones of *Israel, and* will gather the dispersed of *Judah* from the four corners of the earth" (Isaiah 11:10-12). "At that time they shall call Jerusalem 'The Throne of the Lord' " (Jeremiah 3:17).

God will gather Judah *and* Israel. [1] *Together*, they will call Jerusalem "The Throne of the Lord."

Ephraim Will Be Gathered

We have already begun to see the gathering of Judah. But God says of His gathering of the Ephraimite portion of Israel: "How can I give you up, O Ephraim? How can I surrender you, O Israel?....All My compassions are kindled....I will not destroy Ephraim *again*....They will walk after the Lord, he will roar like a lion; indeed he will roar, and his sons will come trembling from the west" (Hosea 11:8-10).

God will not destroy Ephraim again; rather, Ephraim will come from the West, the bastion of Christianity. Ephraim is in the West because God promised an east wind from the Lord would come against him (Hosea 13:15). (An east wind carries to the West.)

Jealousy and Vexation

God says when Ephraim returns, "the envy and jealousy of Ephraim also shall depart, and they who vex and harass Judah from outside or inside shall be cut off; Ephraim shall not envy Judah, and Judah shall not vex and harass Ephraim" (Isaiah 11:13, TAB).

Ephraim is *envious* and *jealous* of Judah. The word is *kanah*, denoting wrath and anger. [2] Surely Ephraim has repeatedly exhibited wrath, even violent anger, toward Judah. Judah, on the other hand, *vexes* and *harasses* Ephraim. This word is *tsarar*, meaning to be an enemy, to distress, to oppress. [3] Over and over again Judah has vexed, even provoked, Ephraim by refusing to acknowledge him as a legitimate heir of Israel. [4]

The day will come when the two houses will no longer exhibit these ugly traits. At that time the people of Ephraim and Judah will unite.

The Two Sticks

God speaks of uniting the two families through the uniting of the "two sticks" that represent them. Speaking of that day, God said: "And you, son of man, take for yourself one stick and write on it, 'For Judah and for the sons of Israel, his companions;' then take another stick and write on it, 'For Joseph, the stick of Ephraim and all the house of Israel, his companions.' Then join them for yourself one to another into one stick, that they may become one in your hand. And when the sons of your people speak to you saying; 'Will you not declare to us what you mean by these?' say to them, 'Thus says the Lord God, "Behold, I will take the stick of Joseph, which is in the hand of *Ephraim*, and the tribes of *Israel*, his companions; and I will put them with it, with the stick of *Judah*, and make them one stick, and they will be one in My hand....I will take the sons of Israel from among the nations where they have gone, and I will gather them from every side and bring them into their own land; and I will make them one nation in the land, on the mountains of Israel; and one king will be king for all of them; and they will no longer be two nations, and they will no longer be divided into two kingdoms. And they will no longer defile themselves with their idols, or with their detestable things, or with any of their transgressions....And they will be My people, and I will be their God...They will *all* have one shepherd...and I will...set My sanctuary in their midst forever. My dwelling place also will be with them; and I will be their God, and they will be My people" ' " (Ezekiel 37:16-27).

An Invincible Army

When Ephraim and Judah are united in God, they will be an invincible army, an army of powerful, prevailing princes fighting the battles of the God of Israel. The *Amplified Bible* says, "But [with united forces] *Ephraim and Judah* will swoop down upon the shoulder of the Philistines' land sloping toward the west; together they will strip the people on the east...They will lay their hand upon Edom and Moab, and the Ammonites shall obey them" (Isaiah 11:14). In that day, God says: "I will bend Judah as My bow, I will fill the bow with Ephraim...Then the Lord will appear over them...and the Lord God will blow the trumpet...The Lord of hosts will defend them...and the Lord their God will save them in that day as the flock of His people; for they are as the stones of a crown, sparkling in His land...For the Lord of hosts has visited His flock, the house of Judah, and will make them like His majestic horse in battle...and they will be as mighty men, treading down the enemy in the mire of the streets in battle; and they will fight, for the Lord will be with them; and the riders on horses will be put to shame. And I shall strengthen the house of Judah, and I shall save the house of Joseph...Ephraim will be like a mighty man, And their heart will be glad as if from wine; indeed, their children will see it and be glad, their heart will rejoice in the Lord. I will whistle for them to gather them together, for I have redeemed them; and they will be as numerous as they were before...They will remember Me in far countries, and they with their children will live and come back. I will bring them back from the land of Egypt, and gather them from Assyria; and I will bring them into the land of Gilead and Lebanon, until no room can be found for them" (Zechariah 9:13-10:10). "And the sons of Judah and the sons of Israel will be gathered together...for great will be the day of Jezreel" (Hosea 1:11).

A Day of Holiness

Great and holy will be the day when God reunites His people. It will be a holy day because God has sworn, "All the sinners of my people will die by the sword" (Amos 9:10). God has declared, "I will remove from your midst your proud, exulting ones. And you will never again be haughty on My holy mountain. But I will leave among you a humble and lowly people, and they will take refuge in the name of the Lord. The remnant of Israel will do no wrong and tell no lies, nor will a deceitful tongue be found in their mouths" (Zephaniah 3:11-13).

God will have His way. He will have an obedient, united House of Israel. He will have an obedient House of Israel that loves Him, His people and His Messiah.

May we, by His grace, prove to be that people.

FOOTNOTES

PUBLISHING INFORMATION FOR ALL BOOKS LISTED CAN BE FOUND IN THE BIBLIOGRAPHY.

-Abbreviations-
ATS   ● *ArtScroll Tanach Series**
BDBL ● *The New Brown-Driver-Briggs-Gesenius Hebrew-Aramaic Lexicon**
NIVSB ● *New International Version Study Bible**
SGL   ● *Strong's Exhaustive Concordance Greek Lexicon**
SHL   ● *Strong's Exhaustive Concordance Hebrew Lexicon**
TWOT ● *Theological Wordbook of the Old Testament**

Chapter One
(1) TWOT #2287.
(2) TWOT #997.
(3) The Bible.

Chapter Two
(1) For a definition of who the angel is, see Genesis 16:7,13; 21:17; 22:11,15-16; 32:29-30; Exodus 3:2; 13:21; 14:19; Daniel 3:25,28; Hosea 12:3-5.
(2) SHL #3290; BDBL #3290; *The Interpreter's Dictionary of the Bible*, Volume 2, pages 782-83.*
(3) SHL #8280; TWOT #2287.
(4) SHL #410; TWOT #93.
(5) *Gesenius' Hebrew-Chaldee Lexicon*, page 370.*
(6) SHL #3478.
(7) BDBL page 975.
(8) TWOT #2287.

(9) *Webster's Third New International Dictionary.*

(10) Since "all Scripture is profitable for doctrine" (2 Timothy 3:16), these verses would also apply to Israelites.

(11) John 4:24.

(12) 1 Chronicles 14:2; 17:14; 28:5; 29:23; 2 Chronicles 9:8; 13:5,8; Isaiah 9:6-7; Luke 1:32-33; Ephesians 5:5; Hebrews 1:3; 3:6; 8:1; 10:12.

Chapter Three

(1) SHL #6509; TWOT #1809; BDBL page 826.

(2) SHL #7235; TWOT #2103.

(3) TWOT #582.

(4) SHL #776; TWOT #167.

(5) SGL #2889.

(6) Luke 19:41; 1 Kings 11:13.

(7) Matthew 27:42; Mark 15:32; John 19:12-13.

(8) Zechariah 8:3; 14:4; Micah 4:2,7.

(9) Genesis 12:2; Exodus 33:13; Joshua 3:17; 4:1; 5:8; Zephaniah 2:9.

(10) SHL #1471; TWOT #326; *Young's Bible Dictionary,* Gentiles, page 230.*

(11) SHL #6951; TWOT #1991.

Chapter Four

(1) *The Evangelical Dictionary of Theology,* page 416.*

(2) *Wycliffe Bible Encyclopedia,* page 609.*

(3) *Unger's Bible Dictionary,* page 367.*

(4) *Zondervan Pictorial Encyclopedia,* Volume 2, page 540.*

(5) *The New Harper's Bible Dictionary,* page 194.* Also see 2 Chronicles 21:3.

(6) *The Interpreter's Dictionary of the Bible,* Volume 2, pages 270-271.*

(7) *Unger's Bible Dictionary,* page 367.*
(8) SHL #4941; TWOT #2443.
(9) *Wycliffe Bible Encyclopedia,* pages 609-610; 843.*
(10) Romans 9:13.

Chapter Five
(1) Genesis 37:5-28. These dreams portray Joseph as a type of the Messiah.
(2) *Unger's Bible Dictionary* says, "Jacob took away the right of primogeniture from Reuben because of his incestuous conduct...and transferred it to Joseph by adopting his two sons" (page 368).*
(3) *Wycliffe Bible Encyclopedia,* page 27.*
(4) *The ArtScroll Tanach Series* is a commentary from Talmudic, Midrashic, and Rabbinic sources.*
(5) ATS, Genesis, Volume 6, page 2098.
(6) Righteous acts.
(7) ATS, Genesis, Volume 6, page 2109.
(8) TWOT says the word "matteh" (stick) "properly means 'staff' or 'rod.' " See word #1352, page 574.
(9) Though Jacob used deception to gain the blessing, Genesis 25:23 makes it clear that God had ordained him as the preeminent one.

Chapter Six
(1) Genesis 41:52; 46:20; 48:1,5,13,14,17,20; 50:23; Numbers 26:28; 1 Chronicles 7:20,22.
(2) 1 Kings 12:21.
(3) *The Kings of Judah and Israel,* by Christopher Knapp, pages 27-28.*
(4) 1 Kings 22:4; 2 Kings 8:18.
(5) 2 Chronicles 11:14 says, "The Levites...came to Judah and Jerusalem, for Jeroboam and his sons had excluded them from serving as priests to the Lord."

However, this does not mean every priest (see 2 Kings 17:28; 1 Kings 12:21, and NIVSB footnote). In addition, there were "those from Ephraim, Manasseh, and Simeon who resided with them." Further, "some men of Asher, Manasseh, and Zebulun...came to Jerusalem" (2 Chronicles 15:9; 30:11). Likewise, Issachar and Zebulun are listed as participants in the Passover of Second Chronicles 30:18. Unfortunately, Judah ultimately fell into the same sins that plagued the Ephraimites. See 2 Kings 16:3; 17:19.

(6) The last war between Israel and Judah was in 735 B.C. See *Chronological Charts of the Old Testament* by John H. Walton, page 62.* Also see 1 Kings 14:30; 15:16; 2 Kings 15:37; 16:5-6.

(7) This number does not include those taken captive by Tiglath-Pileser. The total number of those taken captive remains unknown. The Scriptures allude to a figure as high as 90 percent: "The city that marches out a thousand strong for Israel will have only a hundred left; the town that marches out a hundred strong will have only ten left" (Amos 5:3, NIV; also see 3:12).

(8) NIVSB, page 556. The Assyrian records indicate noble families were taken captive, while agricultural workers were left behind to care for the crops.

(9) NIVSB page 556. "Tiglath-Pileser king of Assyria came and captured Ijon and Abel-beth-maacah and Janoah and Kedesh and Hazor and Gilead and Galilee, all the land of Naphtali; and he carried them captive to Assyria" (2 Kings 15:29). After that, "The king of Assyria brought men from Hamath and Sephar-vaim, and settled them in the cities of Samaria in place of the sons of Israel. So they possessed Samaria [the capital city of Israel] and lived in its cities" (2 Kings 17:24).

(10) *Encyclopaedia Judaica*, Exile, Assyrian, page 1036.*
(11) *Encyclopaedia Judaica*, Ten Lost Tribes, page 1004.*
(12) *Life and Times of Jesus the Messiah*, page 16.*
(13) *Ibid*, page 14.*
(14) *Ibid*, page 15.*

Chapter Seven
(1) SHL #1995; TWOT #505a.
(2) SHL #7235; TWOT #2985.
(3) SHL #505 and 7235.
(4) SHL #6555; TWOT #1826. For a greater understanding of this breaking forth, see *Understanding the Difficult Words of Jesus*, by David Bivin, pages 123-125.*
(5) See Septuagint, *The Zondervan Pictorial Encyclopedia of the Bible*, Volume 5, page 343.*
(6) TWOT #1994. *The Concordance to the Septuagint*, page 433, shows us the translators did this more than 60 times.*
(7) Though culture itself can be the "glue" that holds a people together, it can also hinder. And any and all cultural or traditional values that oppose God's purposes must be denied.
(8) TWOT #1865.
(9) Judges 7:4.
(10) ATS, Genesis, Volume 6, pages 2115-2117.
(11) As translated from *The New Concordance of the Tanach* by Rimona Frank, Hebrew editor.*
(12) ATS, Genesis, Volume 6, page 2121.

Chapter Eight
(1) Verses 43-45 in other translations.
(2) In addition, the tribe of Manasseh came into their land inheritance before the remainder of their brethren did (Joshua 1:14-15). In the same way, many of the

believers in Old Covenant Israel (Manasseh) entered into their heavenly reward before those gathered from the Nations (Ephraim).

(3) *The ArtScroll Tanach Series* says this means God "allowed" Joseph to forget his family. Genesis, Volume 5, page 1809.

(4) SHL #669.

(5) *Gesenius Hebrew Lexicon*, #669, page 73.*

(6) Revelation 11:8; Exodus 1:11-14.

Chapter Ten

(1) Genesis 1:26.

(2) Revelation 22:16; Matthew 1:1; Isaiah 7:14; Revelation 5:5.

(3) See Jesus Christ, *The Interpreter's Dictionary of the Bible*, Volume 2, page 869.*

(4) David said: "You have spoken also of Your servant's house in the far distant future (2 Samuel 7:19, TAB).

(5) King David wanted to build a house for God—a Temple. In response to David's desire to bless God, He promised to build a house for David—a dynasty. This spiritual house would come through the Greater Son of David. (Taken from a cassette tape by Rev. Lindsey, Hebrew Scholar, Pastor, Narkis Street Baptist Church, Jerusalem (See also 1 Chronicles 17).

(6) The throne of David was created for the First-born: "By Him all things were created, both in the heavens and on earth, visible and invisible, whether thrones or dominions or rulers or authorities—all things have been created by Him and for Him" (Colossians 1:16).

(7) SHL #4581; TWOT 1578a.

Chapter Eleven

(1) The Tree is the Cross. See Acts 5:30, KJV.

(2) Anointed One means the Messiah, God's King. See TWOT #1255.

Chapter Twelve

(1) Exodus 12:48-49; Leviticus 19:34; 24:22; Numbers 9:14; 15:15-16,29; Ezekiel 47:22. In addition, see Exodus 12:19; 20:10; 22:21; 23:9,12; Leviticus 17:8,10,12; 18:26; 19:33; 20:2; 22:18; 24:16; 25:6; Numbers 15:30; 35:15; Joshua 20:9; Psalm 146:9; Malachi 3:5.

Chapter Thirteen

(1) This change coincided with the change in the priesthood of Israel—from the Aaronic priesthood to that of Jesus, the High Priest according to the order of Melchizedek (Hebrews 5:6): For "when the priesthood is changed, of necessity there takes place a change of law also" (Hebrews 7:12). Through Messiah's priesthood, Israel's law was changed to that of New Covenant Passover.

(2) Acts 2:41; 4:4.

(3) *The Eternal Church*, by Dr. Bill Hamon, page 79.*

Chapter Fourteen

(1) Isaiah 11:1; Ruth 4:17; Romans 11:18; Revelation 5:5; 22:16.

(2) Romans 11:16-24; Galatians 3:28; Ephesians 2:15.

(3) SGL #1484; SHL #1471.

(4) SGL #4218.

(5) See Gentiles, *Wycliffe Bible Encyclopedia*, page 670.*

(6) SGL #1451.

(7) In Biblical language the heart is the center of life. See Psalm 4:7 and NIVSB note; Proverbs 4:23; Jeremiah 31:33.

(8) Strangers and aliens indicate one who is an acquaintance, a guest, one who lives elsewhere. They differ from sojourners who make their home with the Israelites.

Paul's point is that through the blood of Jesus and heart circumcision, you now hold full citizenship rights in Israel. (See SGL#'s 3581 and 3941, and Foreigner, *The Interpreter's Dictionary of the Bible*, Volume 2, page 310.*

(9) These priests were purchased from every nation, because: "When the most High gave the nations their inheritance, When He separated the sons of man, He set the boundaries of the peoples according to the number of the sons of Israel" (Deuteronomy 32:8).

(10) NIVSB page 1890.

Chapter Fifteen

(1) Hosea, NIVSB, Author and Date.

(2) Jeremiah, NIVSB, Author and Date.

(3) Hosea 1:6,9-10; 2:1,23, and NIVSB footnotes.

(4) SHL #3157; TWOT #582; Hosea 1:4,11, and NIVSB footnotes.

(5) Hosea 8:8; 9:3,17; Amos 7:11; 9:9.

(6) Also see Genesis 22:17; 32:12; Jeremiah 33:22 (plus NIVSB footnote); and Hebrews 11:12.

(7) Judges 3:5-6; Psalm 106:35-36; Hosea 7:11; 8:9-10.

(8) SHL #1104.

(9) On the other hand, countless numbers of Judahites also have been lost among the nations, likewise becoming unidentifiable.

(10) Hosea 1:11; 2:22 (and NIVSB footnotes); Jeremiah 31:27-28; Isaiah 11:11-12.

Chapter Sixteen

(1) Zechariah 10:2; 13:7; Ezekiel 34:12; Matthew 9:36; 26:31.

(2) Also see Matthew 2:6.

(3) These sheep know "the God of peace, who brought up

from the dead the great Shepherd of the sheep through the blood of the eternal covenant, even Jesus our Lord" (Hebrews 13:20).

(4) *Vincent's Word Studies*, Volume II, page 192-193.*

(5) *Exposition of the Gospel of John* by Pink, pages 128-129.*

Chapter Seventeen

(1) NIVSB, Introduction to 1 Kings, pages 464-465.

(2) NIVSB, Introduction to Zechariah, page 1405; The Twelve Prophets, *The Soncino Books of the Bible*, page 267.*

(3) NIVSB, Zechariah 11:14 footnote.

(4) The Twelve Prophets, *The Soncino Books of the Bible*, pages 316-317.*

(5) NIVSB, Introduction to Ezra, page 670.

(6) ATS, Daniel, page 248. In addition, we see that Jesus "came and preached peace to you who were far away and peace to those who were near" (Ephesians 2:17, NIV).

(7) "God...has given the kingship of Israel to David and his descendants forever by a covenant of salt" (2 Chronicles 13:5, NIV). Since Herod was a non-Jew (see NIVSB note, Matthew 2:1), he could not be a fulfillment of this Scripture.

Chapter Eighteen

(1) In their defense, it must be remembered that the multiplied thousands of the early Church were Jewish.

(2) *Controversy of Zion* by Claude Duvernoy pages 96-108; *The Jewish People and Jesus Christ after Auschewitz* by Jacob Jocz, pages 52-78.*

(3) 1 Peter 2:2; Ephesians 4:14-15.

Chapter Nineteen
    (1) 1 Kings 11:31-32; 12:21 and NIVSB footnotes and Joshua 21.
    (2) 1 Samuel 8:11-19; 11:15; 1 Kings 9:15,21, and NIVSB footnotes.

Chapter Twenty
    (1) Genesis 27:4,6,29,33,36-37, and NIVSB footnotes.
    (2) 2 Samuel 19:42-43.
    (3) 2 Chronicles 25:10.

Chapter Twenty-two
    (1) 1 Chronicles 5:2; Isaiah 9:6,7; 11:1-4; Ezekiel 21:27; Daniel 7:14; Luke 1:31-33; and "The Lion of the Tribe of Judah" by Will Varner, August-September issue, *Israel My Glory*, pages 21-22.*
    (2) SGL #3439; *Thayer's Greek Lexicon*, #3439; *The Names Of Christ*, by Frances H. Derk, pages 88-89, 113-114.*
    (3) Teaching tape. Rev. Lindsey, Hebrew Scholar, Pastor, Narkis Street Baptist Church, Jerusalem.
    (4) SHL #5414.

Chapter Twenty-three
    (1) *The Chemistry of the Blood*, page 17.*
    (2) SHL #3722.
    (3) 1 John 1:7; SGL #2511; see forgive, *The Expanded Vines*, page 452.*
    (4) *The Chemistry of the Blood*, page 16.*
    (5) SGL #2675.
    (6) Isaiah 7:14; 9:6-7.
    (7) *The Chemistry of the Blood*, pages 30-31. Italics added.*
    (8) *The New Encyclopaedia Britannica*, Volume 20, page 454, 2b.*

(9) *Webster's Third New International Dictionary*, Volume 1, page 363.*

(10) *Ibid*, Volume 1, page 364.*

(11) *Ibid*, Volume 2, page 1732.*

(12) *Ibid*, Volume 2, page 1825. Italics added.*

(13) We know Jesus had the blood of the Father in His veins because Acts 20:28 speaks of "the church of God which He purchased with His own blood." Therefore, it was "God's...blood."

Chapter Twenty-four

(1) Also see 1 Chronicles 14:2.

(2) This is possibly the reason the king of Egypt said to kill the sons of Israel, but to let the daughters live (Exodus 1:16).

(3) *The New Encyclopaedia Britannica*, 1985 and 1986 Britannica Books of the Year, pages 366 and 369, respectively.*

Chapter Twenty-five

(1) Romans 11:11,KJV; See SGL, stumble, #4417; fall #4098; fall #3900.

(2) However, they did not succeed. See Jeremiah 44:1, 10-11.

(3) Romans 2:12; 4:15; 5:13.

Chapter Twenty-six

(1) Jeremiah 3:18 and NIVSB footnote.

(2) SHL #7065 and 7068; TWOT #2038. This word can also be used in a favorable sense to denote consuming zeal that is focused on one that is loved (see Psalm 69:9).

(3) SHL #6887; TWOT #1974.

(4) Jews put the early Church out of the synagogue and began to recite a curse over them as part of their daily prayer (the Amidah). Even today (perhaps with good reason), Christians find it very difficult to obtain citizenship in Israel.

BIBLIOGRAPHY

The following is a cross reference for books as they are listed in the text and footnotes:

ArtScroll Tanach Series. See Scherman, Nosson.
The Chemistry of the Blood. See DeHaan, M.R.
Chronological Charts of the Old Testament. See Walton, John.
Concordance to the Septuagint. See Hatch, Edwin.
Controversy of Zion. See Duvernoy, Claude.
Encyclopaedia Judaica. See same.
The Eternal Church. See Hamon, Dr. Bill.
The Evangelical Dictionary of Theology. See Elwell, Walter.
The Expanded Vines. See Vine, W.E.
Exposition of the Gospel of John. See Pink, Arthur.
The Interlinear Bible. See Green, Jay.
The Interpreter's Dictionary of the Bible. See same.
The Kings of Judah and Israel. See Knapp, Christopher.
The Lion of the Tribe of Judah. See Varner, Will.
The Life and Times of Jesus the Messiah. See Edersheim, Alfred.
The Names of Christ. See Derk, Francis.
The New Brown-Briggs Lexicon. See Brown, Frances.
The New Concordance of the Tanach. See Even-Shushan, Avraham.
The New Encyclopedia Britannica. See same.
The New Harper's Bible Dictionary. See Miller, Madeline.
Strong's Exhaustive Concordance. See Strong, James.
Thayer's Greek Lexicon. See Thayer, Joseph.

Theological Wordbook of the Old Testament. See Harris, R. Laird.

Gesenius Hebrew Lexicon. See Gesenius' Hebrew Chaldee.

The Twelve Prophets. See Cohen, A.

Unger's Bible Dictionary. See Unger, Merrill.

Understanding the Difficult Words of Jesus. See Bivin, David.

Vincent's Word Studies. See Vincent, Marvin.

Webster's Dictionary. See Webster's Third New.

Wycliffe Bible Encyclopedia. See Pfeiffer, Charles.

Young's Bible Dictionary. See Young, G. Douglas.

Zondervan Pictorial Encyclopedia. See Tenny, Merrill.

The following is a partial listing of the writings that have been of use in the making of this book:

Aharoni, Yohanan; Michael Avi-Yonah. *The Macmillan Bible Atlas, Revised Edition.* 1968, 1977. Macmillan Publishing, Inc. New York.

Barry J. Beitzel. *The Moody Atlas of Bible Lands.* 1985. The Moody Bible Institute. Chicago, Illinois.

Barraclough, Geoffrey. *The Times Atlas of World History.* 1979. Hammond Incorporated. Maplewood, New Jersey.

Bivin, David; Roy Blizzard, Jr. *Understanding the Difficult Words of Jesus.* 1984. Center for Judaic-Christian Studies. Austin, Texas.

Bromiley, G.W., editor. *The International Standard Bible Encyclopedia, Revised Edition.* 4 volumes. 1915, 1979. Wm.B. Eerdman's Publishing Co. Grand Rapids, Michigan.

Brown, Frances, D.D. *The New Brown-Driver-Briggs-Gesenius Hebrew-Aramaic Lexicon.* 1979. Hendrickson Publishers, Inc. Peabody, Massachusetts.

_____ ,*Carta's Historical Atlas Of Israel.* 1983. Carta Publishing. Jerusalem.

Cohen, Rev. Dr. A. "The Twelve Prophets." *The Soncino Books of the Bible*. 1957, 1980. The Soncino Press. London.

DeHann, M.R., M.D. *The Chemistry of the Blood*. 1943, 1971. Zondervan Publishing House. Grand Rapids, Michigan.

Derk, Francis H. *The Names of Christ*. 1969. Bethany Fellowship, Inc. Minneapolis, Minnesota.

Duvernoy, Claude. *Controversy of Zion*. 1987. New Leaf Press. Green Forest, Arkansas.

Edersheim, Alfred. *The Life and Times of Jesus the Messiah*. 1979. Wm. B. Eerdman's Publishing Co. Grand Rapids, Michigan.

_____ , *Encyclopaedia Judaica*. 16 volumes. 1972. Keter Publishing House Ltd. Jerusalem.

Elwell, Walter A., editor. *The Evangelical Dictionary of Theology*. 1984. Baker Book House. Grand Rapids, Michigan.

Even-Shushan, Avraham. *New Concordance of the Tanach*. 1983. Sivan Press Ltd. Jerusalem.

Fay, Frederick L. *A Map Book for Bible Students*. 1966. Fleming H. Revell. Old Tappan, N.J.

Gilbert, Martin. *Atlas of Jewish History*. 1969, 1976. Dorset Press for Steinmatzky Ltd. Jerusalem.

_____ , *Gesenius' Hebrew-Chaldee Lexicon to the Old Testament*. 1979. Baker Book House Company. Grand Rapids, Michigan.

Green, Jay P. Sr. *The Interlinear Bible, Hebrew, Greek, English*. 1976,1979. Baker Book House Company. Grand Rapids, Michigan.

Hamon, Dr. Bill. *The Eternal Church*. 1981. W.S. Hamon, Phoenix, Arizona.

Harris, R. Laird; Gleason L. Archer Jr.; Bruce K. Waltke, editors. *Theological Wordbook of the Old Testament*. 2 volumes. 1980. Moody Press. Chicago.

Hatch, Edwin, M.A., D.D.; Henry A. Redpath, M.A. *Hatch and Redpath Concordance to the Septuagint.* 2 volumes. 1983. Baker Book House. Grand Rapids, Michigan.

Holladay, William L., editor. *A Concise Hebrew And Aramaic Lexicon Of The Old Testament.* 1971. William B. Eerdman's Publishing Company. Grand Rapids, Michigan.

_____ , *The Interpreter's Dictionary of the Bible.* 5 volumes. 1962. Abingdon Press. Nashville, Tennessee.

Jenkins, Simon. *Bible Mapbook.* 1985. Lion Publishing. Herts, England.

Jocz, Jakob. *The Jewish People and Jesus Christ After Auschwitz,* 1981. Baker Book House. Grand Rapids, Michigan.

Josephson, Elmer A. *God's Key to Health And Happiness.* 1962, 1976. Fleming H. Revell Company. Old Tappan, New Jersey.

Knapp, Christopher. *The Kings of Judah & Israel.* 1909, 1983. Loizeaux Brothers Publishers. Neptune, New Jersey.

Lambert, Lance. *Battle for Israel.* 1975. Tyndale House Publishers. Wheaton, Illinois.

Miller, Madeline S.; J. Lane. *New Harper's Bible Dictionary.* 1973. Harper & Row Publishers Inc. New York.

_____ , *The New Encyclopaedia Britannica.* 29 volumes. 1985. Encyclopedia Britannica, Inc. Chicago, Illinois.

_____ , *New International Version Study Bible.* 1985. Zondervan Bible Publishers. Grand Rapids, Michigan.

Pfeiffer, Charles F.; Howard F. Vos; John Rea, editors. *Wycliffe Bible Encyclopaedia.* 1975. The Moody Bible Institute. Chicago, Illinois.

Pink, Arthur W. *Exposition of the Gospel of John.* 1976. Zondervan Publishing House. Grand Rapids, Michigan.

Richards, Lawrence O. *Expository Dictionary of Bible Words.* 1985. Zondervan Publishing House. Grand Rapids, Michigan.

Scherman, Nosson; Meir Zlotowitz, editors. *ArtScroll Tanach Series*. 1977, 1980. Mesorah Publications, Ltd. Brooklyn, New York.

Strong, James LL.D., S.T.D. *The New Strong's Exhaustive Concordance*. 1984. Thomas Nelson Publishers. Nashville, Tennessee.

Tenny, Merrill, editor. *Zondervan Pictorial Encyclopedia of the Bible*. 5 volumes. 1975, 1976. The Zondervan Corporation. Grand Rapids, Michigan.

Terrien, Samuel. *The Golden Bible Atlas*. 1957. Golden Press. Racine, Wisconsin.

Thayer, Joseph Henry, D.D. *Thayer's Greek-English Lexicon of the New Testament*. 1977. Baker Book House Company. Grand Rapids, Michigan.

Thomas, Robert L., Th.D., editor. *New American Standard Exhaustive Concordance Of The Bible*. 1981. Holman Bible Publishers. Nashville, Tennessee.

Thomas, Dr. Winton, editor. *Documents from Old Testament Times*. 1958, 1961. Harper & Row. New York.

Turner, Nigel. *Christian Words*. 1981. Thomas Nelson Publishers. Nashville, Tennessee.

Unger, Merrill F. *Unger's Bible Dictionary*. 1957, 1966. The Moody Bible Institute. Chicago, Illinois.

Varner, Will. "The Lion of the Tribe of Judah". August-September issue, *Israel My Glory*. Bellmawr, New Jersey.

Vincent, Marvin R., D.D. *Vincent's Word Studies of the New Testament*. 4 volumes. Macdonald Publishing Company. McLean, Virginia.

Vine, W.E. *The Expanded Vine's Expository Dictionary of New Testament Words*. 1984. Bethany House Publishers. Minneapolis, Minnesota.

Walton, John H. *Chronological Charts of the Old Testament*. 1978. Zondervan Publishing House. Grand Rapids, Michigan.

_____ , *Webster's Third New International Dictionary.* 3 volumes. 1981. Encyclopaedia Britannica, Inc. Chicago, Illinois.

Whiston, William, A.M., translator, *The Works Of Flavius Josephus.* 4 volumes. 1974. Baker Book House. Grand Rapids, Michigan.

Wilson, William. *Wilson's Old Testament Word Studies, Unabridged Edition.* Macdonald Publishing Co. McLean, Virginia.

Young, G. Douglas, Ph.D. *Young's Bible Dictionary.* 1984. Masada Press. Tyndale House Publishers, Inc. Wheaton, Illinois.

Young, Robert, LL.D. *Young's Analytical Concordance to the Bible.* 1982. Thomas Nelson Publishers. Nashville, Tennessee.

INDEX

LET THE ONE WHO IS TAUGHT THE WORD SHARE ALL GOOD THINGS WITH HIM WHO TEACHES (GALATIANS 6:6).

IF THROUGH THIS BOOK THE SPIRIT OF GOD HAS ACCOMPLISHED A GOOD THING IN YOUR LIFE, PLEASE WRITE AND TELL ME ABOUT YOUR BLESSING.

BATYA WOOTTEN
HOUSE OF DAVID
BOX 777
LAKEWOOD, NEW YORK 14750

THE KINGDOM OF DAVID
CA. 990 to 968 B.C.

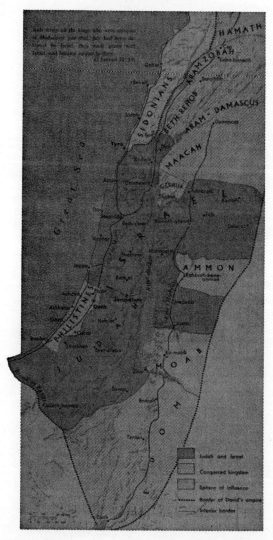

Reprinted with permission of Macmillan Publishing Company from the *Macmillan Bible Atlas, Revised Edition*, by Yohanan Aharoni and Michael Avi-Yonah. Copyright: 1964, 1966, 1968 by Carta Ltd.

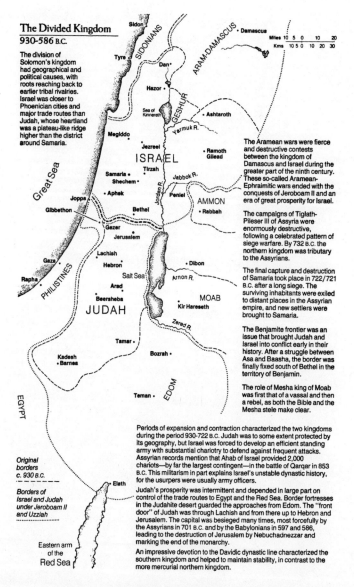

The Divided Kingdom
930-586 B.C.

The division of Solomon's kingdom had geographical and political causes, with roots reaching back to earlier tribal rivalries. Israel was closer to Phoenician cities and major trade routes than Judah, whose heartland was a plateau-like ridge higher than the district around Samaria.

Sidon

SIDONIANS

Damascus

ARAM-DAMASCUS

Miles 10 5 0   10   20
Kms 10 5 0 10 20 30

Tyre

Dan

Hazor

GESHUR

Sea of Kinnereth

Ashtaroth

Megiddo

Yarmuk R.

Jezreel

Ramoth Gilead

ISRAEL

Tirzah

Samaria

Shechem

Jabbok R.

Aphek

Jordan R.

Peniel

AMMON

Joppa

Bethel

Rabbah

Gibbethon

Gezer

Jerusalem

Great Sea

Lachish

Hebron

Dibon

Salt Sea

Arnon R.

Arad

Gaza

Rapha

PHILISTINES

Beersheba

JUDAH

Kir Hareseth

MOAB

Zered R.

Tamar

Kadesh Barnea

Bozrah

Teman

EDOM

EGYPT

Original borders c. 930 B.C.

Borders of Israel and Judah under Jeroboam II and Uzziah

Elath

Eastern arm of the Red Sea

The Aramean wars were fierce and destructive contests between the kingdom of Damascus and Israel during the greater part of the ninth century. These so-called Aramean-Ephraimitic wars ended with the conquests of Jeroboam II and an era of great prosperity for Israel.

The campaigns of Tiglath-Pileser III of Assyria were enormously destructive, following a celebrated pattern of siege warfare. By 732 B.C. the northern kingdom was tributary to the Assyrians.

The final capture and destruction of Samaria took place in 722/721 B.C. after a long siege. The surviving inhabitants were exiled to distant places in the Assyrian empire, and new settlers were brought to Samaria.

The Benjamite frontier was an issue that brought Judah and Israel into conflict early in their history. After a struggle between Asa and Baasha, the border was finally fixed south of Bethel in the territory of Benjamin.

The role of Mesha king of Moab was first that of a vassal and then a rebel, as both the Bible and the Mesha stele make clear.

Periods of expansion and contraction characterized the two kingdoms during the period 930-722 B.C. Judah was to some extent protected by its geography, but Israel was forced to develop an efficient standing army with substantial chariotry to defend against frequent attacks. Assyrian records mention that Ahab of Israel provided 2,000 chariots—by far the largest contingent—in the battle of Qarqar in 853 B.C. This militarism in part explains Israel's unstable dynastic history, for the usurpers were usually army officers.

Judah's prosperity was intermittent and depended in large part on control of the trade routes to Egypt and the Red Sea. Border fortresses in the Judahite desert guarded the approaches from Edom. The "front door" of Judah was through Lachish and from there up to Hebron and Jerusalem. The capital was besieged many times, most forcefully by the Assyrians in 701 B.C. and by the Babylonians in 597 and 586, leading to the destruction of Jerusalem by Nebuchadnezzar and marking the end of the monarchy.

An impressive devotion to the Davidic dynastic line characterized the southern kingdom and helped to maintain stability, in contrast to the more mercurial northern kingdom.

Exile of Northern Kingdom

Miles	0		100		200		300
Kms	0	100	200	300	400		

Taken from *The New International Version Study Bible*. Copyright 1985 by the Zondervan Corporation. Used by permission.

THE EXILE TO AND FROM ISRAEL
IN THE DAYS OF TIGLATH-PILESER III
712 B.C.

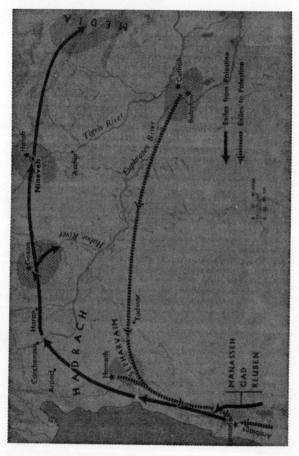

The Ephraimites were scattered throughout Assyria. Babylonians were then moved to Samaria in their place. Reprinted with permission of Macmillan Publishing Company from the *Macmillan Bible Atlas, Revised Edition*, by Yohanan Aharoni and Michael Avi-Yonah. Copyright: 1964, 1966, 1968 by Carta Ltd.

The dispersions of the Northern and Southern Kingdoms

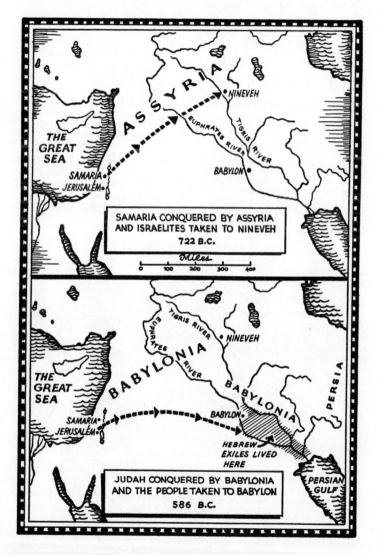

From *A Map Book For Bible Students* by Frederick L. Fay. Published by Whittemore's. Used by permission.

THE EXILE FROM JUDAH
597 to 582 B.C.

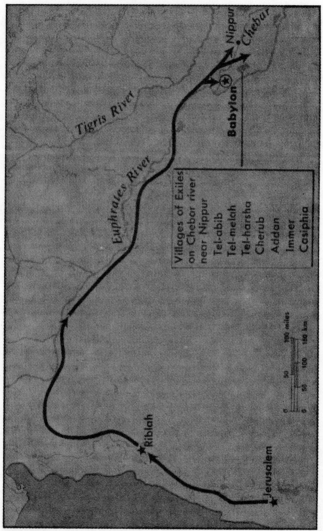

Villages of Exiles
on Chebar river
near Nippur

Tel-abib
Tel-melah
Tel-harsha
Cherub
Addan
Immer
Casiphia

Nippur

Chebar

Babylon

Tigris River

Euphrates River

Riblah

Jerusalem

Reprinted with permission of Macmillan Publishing Company from
the *Macmillan Bible Atlas, Revised Edition,* by Yohanan Aharoni
and Michael Avi-Yonah. Copyright: 1964, 1966, 1968 by Carta Ltd.

Only a remnant returned from Babylon

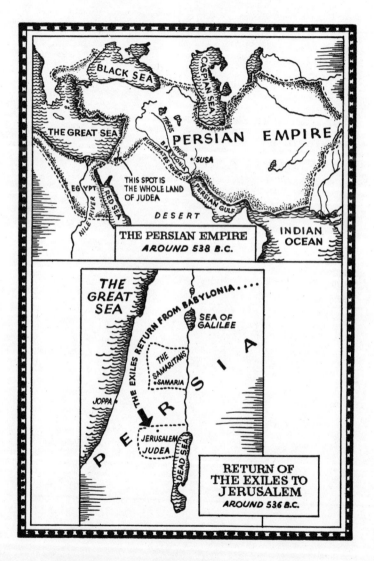

From *A Map Book For Bible Students* by Frederick L. Fay.
Published by Whittemore's. Used by permission.

THE RETURN TO ZION
538 to 445 B.C.

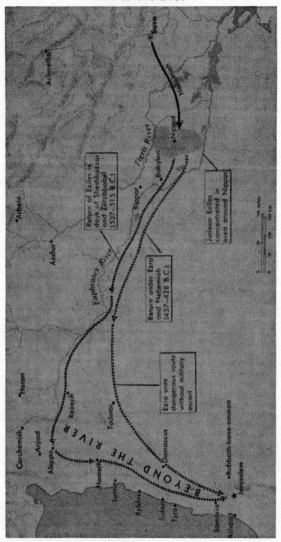

Reprinted with permission of Macmillan Publishing Company from the *Macmillan Bible Atlas, Revised Edition,* by Yohanan Aharoni and Michael Avi-Yonah. Copyright: 1964, 1966, 1968 by Carta Ltd.

Millions of physical Israelites have been assimilated into the Church

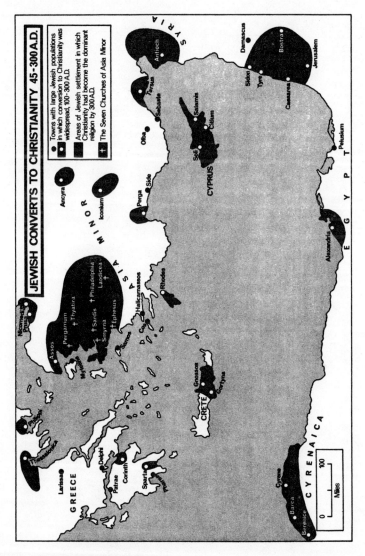

From *Atlas of Jewish History* by Martin Gilbert. Published by Steimatzky. Used by permission.

PALESTINE IN THE VISION OF EZEKIEL
Ezek. 47:13 — 48:29